ASIAN HERBS & VEGETABLES

How *to* identify, grow and
use *them* in Australia

PENNY WOODWARD

HYLAND HOUSE

To Dad
my guide, my inspiration, my friend

Acknowledgements

Many people helped me with the writing of this book, but none more so than Rose-Marie Lacherez who gave me advice, information, friendship, access to her garden and wonderful meals. Thanks also to Clive Blazey of Digger's Seeds, Professor H.F. Chin and Yoshitaka Kamikura who have allowed me to use their photographs. Also thank you to Basil Natoli, co-ordinator of several Community Gardens in central Melbourne, Isabell Shipard of Shipard's Herb Nursery, Frances and Jeff Michaels of Green Harvest, and Peter and Sue de Vaus of New Gippsland Seeds, who all allowed me access to their gardens to photograph plants. I am also grateful for the hard work of Michael and Kylie at Hyland House, and to Pauline McClenahan for the inspired design of the book. As with my other books, this one would not have been possible without my husband Tony, who reads my manuscripts, looks after our children and cooks meals while I'm working. Thank you too to Ellen and Dan who are so tolerant of my absences, both mental and physical, when I am totally absorbed in writing or photography.

Hyland House Publishing Pty Ltd
PO Box 122, Flemington, Victoria 3031

Copyright © Penny Woodward 2000

National Library of Australia Cataloguing-in-publication data:

Woodward, Penny.

Asian herbs and vegetables: how to identify, grow and use them in Australia.

Includes index.
ISBN 1 86447 074 7.
1. Herb gardening - Australia. 2. Vegetable gardening - Australia. 3. Vegetables - Asia. I. Title.
635.0994

Design and layout by Pauline McClenahan, Captured Concepts
Edited by Bet Moore
Produced by Phoenix Offset

Front cover (top to bottom):
lemon grass (page 64), bird's eye pepper (page 50), pickled rakkyo bulbs (page 11)

Contents

Common name key to Contents

Introduction

The term 'Asian herbs and vegetables' describes a wide array of plants that are grown by Asian people and used by them in varying ways in what is loosely known as 'Asian cuisine'. In Australia, the demand for Asian ingredients, including herbs and vegetables, has grown in the last 10 years for several reasons. Ethnic diversity has increased. There has also been a greater emphasis on healthy foods, and the desire for added variety or something 'new' now drives many consumer choices. The purpose of this book is to introduce people from Western backgrounds to some of these 'new' herbs and vegetables and their associated panoply of new flavours, textures, shapes and scents. *Asian Herbs and Vegetables* makes it possible to identify and grow these herbs and vegetables and suggests some of the ways they can be used.

What is an Asian herb or vegetable? It is difficult to pinpoint because there is such diversity, but there are some common themes. Many of the plants are tropical in origin, many are aquatic in origin and many are strongly flavoured. In selecting plants for this book I have worked within certain constraints. All the plants described are used in the cuisines of Asia, they are available (sometimes with some difficulty) in Australia, and they can be grown in the average garden in most parts of Australia. Some herbs and vegetables that are common in European cuisine are also used in Asia, but most are not included in this book because the details of how to grow and use them are clearly set out in numerous other books. They include vegetables such as beans, sweet pepper, melons and squashes, and herbs like parsley. Some vegetables, like eggplants and capsicums that are also commonly used in European cooking, have been included because Asian cooks use an unusual form or use them in a different way.

Although this book is titled *Asian Herbs and Vegetables*, some plants that are more usually classified as spices are also included. This is because they are often also used as vegetables or herbs. Also, I have not tried to separate plants into categories of use like spice, herb or vegetable because the same plant is often used in different ways in different dishes, sometimes as a flavouring and other times as a major ingredient. Similarly, I have not grouped plants according to the part used (leaf, root, fruit) because with many of the plants, all parts are used.

When trying to define an Asian vegetable I had discussions with many people about the definition of Asia. Under the *Encyclopaedia Britannica* definition 'Asia' includes such countries as Israel, Siberia, Turkey, Saudi Arabia, Iran, Iraq, India, Bangladesh and Pakistan. The cuisines and culinary traditions of these countries vary markedly from those of China, Japan and South-East Asia. There is a common thread in the culinary traditions of China, Japan and South-East Asia, partly caused by the climate and partly by the presence of Chinese immigrants, whose culinary traditions have been incorporated into the various national cuisines. Indian cultural and culinary influences have also permeated China, Japan and South-East Asia over many centuries, so numerous plants used in India have been adopted to a greater or lesser extent. For this reason, several plants that originate in India are also included. In this book then, the countries included in the term 'Asia' are Burma, China, Indonesia, Japan, Kampuchea, Laos, Malaysia, Philippines, Singapore, South and North Korea, Taiwan, Thailand and Vietnam.

The lifestyle in many parts of Asia is still predominantly rural in character, with nearly every family growing their own vegetables and herbs, while the tradition in Asian cities is to also use fresh ingredients. Most people still shop every day at one of the fresh food markets to obtain the ingredients for the evening meal. Fresh vegetables and herbs thus play a much larger role in Asian lives than they do in Western lives. In Asia, the climate varies from cooler temperate to equatorial, with all the variations in between. This allows for an interesting range of plants to be grown. Combine this with the population's dependence on rice, which must be grown in water, and it is no surprise that many of their cultivated plants are grown in or near water.

In rural communities and in cities, meat is often hard to obtain, or expensive, so vegetables must be selected not only for taste, texture and variety, but also for protein content as they are the main source of protein. It follows that many of the root vegetables and some of the leafy and pod-bearing vegetables used in Asia are high in protein. Not only could these add variety to our diets, but they could become increasingly important to the large numbers of vegetarians in our society who are keen to try other meat substitutes.

The countries from which these plants come vary in latitude from approximately 10°S to 50°N. The only exception to this are the remote northern parts of China. Australia falls in between the latitudes of about 10°S to 45°S, and this means much of our climate, especially on the coast, is similar to Asia's, apart from the equatorial zones. Although many of the plants described are tropical plants, they can often be grown in subtropical and temperate regions with a little extra care.

Culinary herbs and vegetables divide roughly into three groups delineated by the part used. These are roots, fruits and leaves (this last includes leafy herbs). As mentioned before, many of the plants described fit into all three groups as all parts are used. Leafy vegetables are some of the easiest to grow and to obtain. They are also a very important component of the diet. All are high in dietary fibre while being low in carbohydrates and fat. Many are also the equivalent of multivitamin tablets containing vitamins A, B complex and C as well several minerals including calcium and iron. Where possible I have listed, in the Use sections for each plant, those vitamins and minerals the plants contain. Dark green leaves are usually more nutritious than pale green or yellow ones, and the younger the leaves are, the more tender and easily digestible they are. Some leaves contain dangerous alkaloids, oxalic acid, nitrates or hydrocyanic acid. Where applicable, I have pointed this out in the Use section. Generally, cooking dissipates or destroys these poisons, so if in doubt always cook first and throw away the water.

Root vegetables are often more difficult to grow and take longer to mature than leafy vegetables. They have the benefit, however, of a much longer storage life and many also contain, in addition to high levels of protein, large quantities of the starch essential to provide bulk in the diet. Some roots are also important flavour sources. Fruits too, often take

longer to grow than leafy vegetables, but they provide flavour, dietary fibre and protein, as well as vitamins and minerals.

Of the 94 plants described in this book more than 60 fall into only nine family groups. Often plants within these groups are used in similar ways. These nine families are the Asteraceae, Alliaceae, Apiaceae, Fabaceae, Lamiaceae, Brassicaceae, Solanaceae, Cucurbitaceae and Zingiberaceae.

The Asteraceae includes leafy greens like burdock and garland chrysanthemum, the Apiaceae the herbs like dill, leaf celery and coriander and the Lamiaceae some of the aromatic leafy herbs like mints and basils. The other families include most of the vegetables.

The cultivated species of Brassicaceae are very important to horticulture. This family contains some 40 species (and countless cultivars) of annual and biennial plants. It includes our well-known cabbages, broccoli and cauliflower. But in this group are also some of the better

known leafy Asian vegetables — plants like Chinese cabbage, Chinese white cabbage, Chinese broccoli to name but a few. Brassicaceae is a very perplexing and confusing family taxonomically. This is because natural crosses between groups often result in viable hybrids, and also because new cultivars are actively being developed by science.

In the Fabaceae are all the important leguminous bean and pea crops, many of which are high in protein and so essential to the Asian diet. These legumes are also high in vitamin B, and the sprouted seed high in vitamin C. They have the added benefit of improving the soil in which they are grown because bacteria in their root nodules fix nitrogen, making it available for other plants.

Garlic, onions and chives are found in the Alliaceae, and this family, combined with the Zingiberaceae, which includes ginger and Chinese keys, provides many of the stronger flavours found in Asian cooking. They are also widely used medicinally.

The Solanaceae is another family that includes some very important economic crops. They mostly grow as shrubs or small trees. The leaves of many of the plants in this family contain an alkaloid called solanine which is poisonous. So as a general rule, leaves from plants in this family should not be eaten. Plants included in this group are eggplants and capsicums.

The final family is the Cucurbitaceae. In this group we find all the pumpkins, marrows, gourds and melons. These common names, especially gourd and melon, are often used interchangeably but all the gourds, melons, pumpkins and marrows described in this book are used as vegetables rather than as fruits. So they are more similar to, say, zucchini than they are, for instance, to watermelon. Many of these vegetables supply bulk and fibre to the diet, as well as some vitamins and minerals, but they are not high in protein.

Plants are listed in alphabetical order of their botanical names so that closely related plants like the brassicas can all be dealt with in the same section. An extensive index makes it possible to quickly locate any plant. To maximise the probability of identifying plants that are being used in Asian cooking, one or more photographs accompany every plant described. As a further aid to identification I have included as many of the Asian names for these plants as possible — the Chinese names are spelt phonetically of course. Often the English version of an Asian name will be spelt in several different ways, and some of these variants have also been included. The English names I have used are those most commonly used in Australia and/or those that are least likely to cause confusion. For instance I have used the name Chinese white cabbage instead of bok choy for plants in

Brassica rapa Chinensis Group because plants in *Brassica rapa* Pekinensis Group are also called bok choy. My primary reference for the botanical names has been *The New Royal Horticultural Society Dictionary of Gardening.*

I have grown most of the plants described in this book. I have relied on the advice of other experienced gardeners to provide the growth details of those plants I have not been able to grow. Even with this advice not all the cultural particulars for all plants are as detailed as I would like. As these plants become more popular and more widely used in Australia, this information will become more readily available. I would be interested to hear from anyone who has grown these plants and feels they have information that could expand the knowledge base of this book.

Although I have wide and varied experience as a gardener, I do not regard myself as a good cook. For this reason the main emphasis of *Asian Herbs and Vegetables* is on identifying and growing these plants. I have indicated which parts of the plants are used, and have given some suggestions as to how they can be used, but it is beyond the scope of this book to provide detailed recipes. Recipe books from different cultures are marked with an asterisk in the list of References and Further Reading (see page 138). It is also possible, with a little imagination, to use these herbs and vegetables in recipes with a more Western orientation. A starting point for someone with no experience of Asian vegetables would be to substitute an Asian vegetable for a Western one. Try using Chinese cabbage instead of ordinary cabbage in a coleslaw. The flavour is milder and sweeter. Or substitute young edible bottle gourds or chokos for zucchini. The next step would be to add one or two more unusual Asian vegetables, maybe snake bean and garlic chive flower buds, in a favourite vegetable stir-fry. Once confidence is gained the possibilities are endless.

Since the earliest times, people have gathered their vegetables and flavourings from plants growing around them in their environment. Today it is not possible to do this on anything but a very minor scale. These days many people have a greater interest in food but less time to indulge that interest. Exotic dishes can be produced with an increase in time and energy or we can add to the variety of tastes, textures and aromas in our food through a wider choice of ingredients. Asian herbs and vegetables provide this variety but can be used in such a way that they take very little time to prepare. European migration to Australia after the Second World War altered forever the way we eat. Asian migration is in the process of doing the same thing. An exciting era of adventurous eating is beginning to unfold. We are fortunate that we already have a huge array of interesting herbs and vegetables available in our local markets. These are usually found only in the centre of big cities and only some of the herbs and vegetables discussed in this book have found their way to these markets. I hope that, with the help of *Asian Herbs and Vegetables*, everyone will now be able to grow these herbs and vegetables and so expand the range of flavours and foods available, no matter where they live in Australia.

Abbreviations

Bu	Burmese
ChC	Cantonese Chinese
ChH	Hokkien Chinese
ChM	Mandarin Chinese
In	Indonesian
Ja	Japanese
Kh	Khmer
Ko	Korean
La	Laotian
Ma	Malaysian
Ph	Pilipino
Th	Thai
Vi	Vietnamese

Abelmoschus esculentus Malvaceae
syn. *Hibiscus esculentus*

okra, gombo, gumbo, lady's fingers, bindi

kok-tau (ChC); jiao dou (ChM); kopi arab, kebang dapros (In); okura, america-neri (Ja); tuah lek (La); kacang bendi (Ma); saluyota bunga (Ph); kachieb, grajee-ap morn (Th); dau bab (Vi)

Indigenous to Africa and India, okra has been used in Egypt for centuries. It was carried from Egypt to Europe and then to the Far East. Okra found its way to the New World in the 17th century, probably on slave ships. It is now widely grown throughout Asia and other tropical regions.

Description Okra is an erect annual that grows as a shrub to about 2 m. The whole plant is covered in fine hairs, the stems are woody and the leaves three to five lobed. Flowers are sulphur-yellow with a deep red eye. The dark green fruit are elongated, ridged, pointed at one end and 10 – 20 cm long. The fruit is very mucilaginous and contains many round dark green, brown, black or white seeds. If the fruit is not harvested it dries out and splits into five parts. There are now several different cultivars available that vary in height, fruit and flower colour and cold tolerance.

Cultivation Okra does best in direct sunlight and will tolerate the strong summer sun in southern Australia. It grows in most soils as long as they are well-drained, but prefers slightly acid soil (pH 6–6.5) that has been prepared with generous additions of organic matter. Okra will not survive a frost, so plant after the last chance of frost is over — from spring to early summer in cooler regions. In the tropics it can be planted from late winter to late summer. It grows easily from seed, as long as soil temperatures are over 15°C (optimum soil temperature is about 26°C). Seed germinates more readily if it has been soaked for 12 hours first. Place on damp cotton wool and only plant the seeds that have begun to swell. Place seeds about 2 cm deep and 30 – 40 cm apart, with about 1 m between rows (although most families would only need a few plants). Okra does best if a fertiliser rich in phosphorus is added to the soil just before planting, and again when the pods begin to grow (try using wood ash

combined with rotted horse or cow manure). If plants have too much nitrogen there will be prolific leaf growth at the expense of the pods. Water regularly during dry weather and mulch around plants to preserve moisture.

The first fruits will be ready to pick about 10 weeks after planting. They are at their best when they are still immature and about 8 cm long. Wear gloves when picking as spines on the fruit can irritate the skin of some people who are sensitive to them. Washing removes the irritating spines, or try some of the spineless cultivars available such as 'Clemsons Spineless'. This cultivar grows well in cooler climates. If fruit are left on the plant for too long they become fibrous and unpalatable. Remove any fruits that have grown too big as this will encourage new fruits to grow — but at the end of the season leave a few fruit to fully mature to provide seed for next year's crop.

Use Immature fresh green fruits, either whole or chopped, can be steamed, blanched or stir-fried and eaten as a vegetable. They taste a little like oysters but the taste is mild, so they are often added to stronger flavoured foods. The best way to eat okra as a vegetable is to fry whole, with a small part of the stem attached, in a little oil for a few minutes. Okra can be something of an acquired taste when the mucilage is released. This happens when the fruit is cut or after prolonged cooking. Try adding okra to curries, stews, soups and gravies, but only in the last few minutes, unless the mucilaginous texture is an important part of the dish. Young fruits are high in vitamin C, carotene, calcium, magnesium, potassium and phosphate. They also contain smaller amounts of thiamine, riboflavin and vitamin B6. Fruits freeze well for later use. Young shoots and leaves, flower buds and flowers can also be eaten, usually steamed, and an edible oil is extracted from the ripe seeds.

Abelmoschus manihot Malvaceae

Tree spinach, hibiscus spinach, ibika, aibika

Kapas hutan (Ma)

Tree spinach is closely related to okra and musk mallow (*A. moschatus*). Musk mallow is an ornamental grown for its colourful flowers, while tree spinach is grown more for its edible leaves. Tree spinach is a native of South-East Asia and is widely grown in the tropics.

Description Tree spinach can grow as tall as 2 m but it is usually smaller. It has a strong central stem with large, attractive, glossy, green leaves that are more or less deeply divided. In late summer, yellow or white hibiscus-like flowers grow and are followed by angled pods.

Cultivation Grow tree spinach from seed, sown either in pots or where it is to grow. Place seed about 2 cm deep and 40 cm apart, in rows 1 m apart. Tree spinach likes a relatively rich, well-composted soil, good drainage and lots of sunlight. Water regularly or the leaves may become tough. Plants are frost-tender, so in cooler regions only plant out once the last chance of frost is over in spring. In the tropics, plant any time from late winter to autumn. Start harvesting leaves as soon as the plants are big enough.

Use The large leaves are used in salads, stir-fries, stews and soup. If they are going

to be cooked, then do so for no more than five minutes or the leaves will become slimy. Leaves are high in protein and contain iron, potassium, magnesium and calcium.

Allium cepa (Aggregatum Group) Alliaceae

Shallots, echalote

Chung tu (Ch); bawang mera (In); ktim krahaam (Kh); houa phak boua (La); bawang merah (Ma); hua hom, horm lek, horm daeng (Th); hanh cu, khan kho (Vi)

Shallots have been grown for centuries in many different countries and are now widely grown in both Asia and Europe. They came to Australia with the First Fleet in 1788 and commercial crops are now grown in New South Wales, Tasmania and Victoria.

Description Shallots grow from a single bulb that will divide into up to 20 segments as the shallots grow. Each segment produces tubular green leaves up to 40 cm in height. If the bulbs are not harvested then white flower heads may appear at the end of the season or in the second year. Shallots used in Asia usually have a purple or reddish skin and are often smaller than those seen in Europe. This perennial form of the common onion, grown mainly for its bulbs, should not be confused with the annual or spring onions which are also sometimes called shallots.

Cultivation Shallots are usually grown by planting individual bulbs, as plants rarely flower and/or produce fertile seed. Plant shallot bulbs any time from autumn to early spring, with half the bulb pro-

truding from the soil. Space them about 40 cm apart in rows the same distance apart. They like a sunny, open position and fertile, well-drained soil with a pH over 6.5. Shallots do best if the soil has a high potash content and is not too high in nitrogen. New bulbs are only reliably formed at daytime maximums over 20°C and long days are needed to trigger bulb growth. Lift bulbs when the leaves begin to wither in late summer and autumn, and dry by hanging in bunches in a dry airy place out of direct light. Pick green leaves as soon as plants are big enough, but take care not to remove the central growing stalk. Shallots do not grow well in the tropics because the warm humid summers cause them to rot, and in winter, although the climate is more suitable, the days are not long enough to trigger bulb growth.

Use Both the bulbs and leaves are eaten. Bulbs are added to stir-fries with many different meats and vegetables. They are also an important component of pastes used for seasoning. For example, in Malaysia the paste known as *rempah*, and in Indonesia the paste known as *bumbu*, both have shallots as an important ingredient. Shallots are preferred to other onions in these pastes, because their flavour is sweeter and, as they contain less moisture, they can be fried without becoming stewed. This alters the flavour. Shallots are also chopped and added to salads, are an important ingredient of stir-fries, and in Vietnam, are deep-fried until crisp and then used as a garnish. Leaves are also used as a garnish, and can be added to salads and stir-fries just before serving.

Allium chinense Alliaceae

Rakkyo, Baker's garlic, Chinese scallions, Japanese scallions

Tsung tao, k'iu t'au (ChC); jiao tou, ch'iao t'ou, ku jiao, (ChM); namemira, rakkyo (Ja)

Rakkyo is indigenous to central-eastern China and was probably first cultivated there. One of the earliest written references to rakkyo comes from the Han dynasty (206 BC – AD 220); several cooking methods are recorded in a book of manners from that era, but it has been used medicinally for much longer. Today,

rakkyo is still found growing wild in the mountainous regions of eastern China and less commonly in northern India. It is cultivated extensively in Japan and in central and southern parts of China, and to a lesser extent on some Pacific Islands. Both China and Japan export hundreds of tonnes of pickled rakkyo bulbs.

Description Rakkyo grows as a dense clump of narrow, tubular, thin-walled leaves, that closely resemble chives (*A. schoenoprasum*), except that rakkyo leaves are not as erect. They are bright green instead of blue-green, and in cross-section they are three to five angled instead of circular. The bulbs are small, narrow, ovoid in shape and usually asymmetrical. In cross-section they are made up of concentric rings like onion bulbs. The bulbs form a dense clump with about three leaves to each bulb. Leaves die back in midsummer, and in late summer or autumn solid flower stalks emerge from the centre of the old leaves. New leaves appear at the same time or soon after, but these grow from new lateral bulbs. Nodding, rose-pink to lavender coloured flowers occur in groups of 15 – 20 on each flower stalk.

Cultivation Rakkyo is always cultivated by planting bulbs because it never produces fertile seed. Plant bulbs in late summer or autumn just below the soil surface about 20 cm apart. Grow in any reasonably light, well-drained soil in full sun. Dig in some compost and well-rotted manure a few weeks before planting, and add some good general fertiliser when the bulbs are planted. Keep bulbs watered during dry periods, but otherwise rakkyo is a fairly tough plant that doesn't need a lot of attention. Rakkyo will also grow well if interplanted with other crops. If harvesting the bulbs to pickle, then dig them up after the leaves have died back in summer. If growing them to use the fresh bulbs and white stems, then harvest bulbs one or two months earlier in early summer — before they die back. Rakkyo, like other bulb-forming onion plants, does not grow well in tropical regions.

Use It is the egg-shaped bulb of rakkyo that is generally used. Some bulbs are pickled in salt, soy sauce and sugar, or in sugar alone (see front cover). Bulbs can also be used as a relish in curry dishes or eaten fresh. The taste and texture of rakkyo is difficult to describe, but its main characteristics are the crisp texture of both fresh and pickled bulbs and the strong, distinctive, but basically onion-like, flavour. The strong taste and flavour make fresh rakkyo an acquired taste. In Japan, rakkyo is often marketed as "shallots".

Photograph by Yoshitaka Kamikura

12

Allium fistulosum Alliaceae

Japanese bunching onion, evergreen bunching onion, welsh onion

taai tsung, tsung (ChC); qing cong, da cong, feng cong, xiao cong (ChM); bawang daun (In); atasuki, negi (Ja); bawang daun (Ma); ton horm (Th); hanh (Vi)

This onion has been cultivated since prehistoric times and was the main garden onion of China and Japan. It is mentioned in Chinese literature as early as 100 BC and in Japan by AD 918. Over the centuries many variants have been selected and grown and their uses have been wide ranging. The array of Japanese bunching onion cultivars in Asia is probably as diverse as that of the bulb onion in Europe and America. In China, Japan and many other Asian countries, Japanese bunching onions are still the most important onion crop. In Western cultures, Japanese bunching onion cultivars have been crossed with *Allium cepa* cultivars to produce a range of larger spring onions. These cultivars are grown commercially.

Description There are two main varieties of bunching onion grown commercially in Asia. One is the short bunching onion that consists of bunches of short stems and very tender leaves. This includes cultivars such as 'Kyoto Market', 'Asagi Bunching' and 'Evergreen' which are grown mainly for their leaves. The second variety is the long bunching onion which is grown for its long blanched stem (similar to leeks). These varieties have tougher leaves and often grow through winter. Cultivars include 'Kiyotaki', 'Tsukuba' and 'Ishikura'. There are also many cultivars that are grown as spring onions.

Japanese bunching onions are perennial onions that grow in large, robust, perennial clumps from a short rhizome with tapering roots. These onions have no obvious bulb but, like the leek, are grown for their thickened stems, which are made of elongated leaf bases. Each plant produces a hollow stem with two to six hollow cylindrical leaves. Many Japanese bunching onions multiply at the base, producing numerous side-shoots. Clumps usually remain green all winter, although some cultivars will yellow or die back. In the second year, and every following year, each plant produces a globular head of yellowish-white flowers.

Cultivation Bunching onions can be grown all over Australia from very cold mountainous regions to the tropics. In more southern regions, where days are longer, leaf growth is promoted and flowering discouraged. Conversely very cold temperatures may cause plants to flower and set seed prematurely. Bunching onions grow best in well-drained sandy loams with added organic matter and additional phosphate, but onion plants don't like fresh manure so make sure any used is well-rotted. If the soil is heavy clay then try raising the bed in which they are to grow. Bunching onions prefer neutral to slightly alkaline soils (6.5–7.5) and full sun, will tolerate fairly dry conditions but don't like to be waterlogged.

Grow new plants from seed that is best sown in trays or seed beds and later transplanted, although they will grow from seed sown directly into the garden. Seed germinates most readily at soil temperatures of 15° – 25°C. Plant seeds just below the surface of the soil, and when the seedlings are big enough to transplant (a few centimetres high) they can be moved to the position they are to grow. Short bunching types are planted in trenches about 5 cm deep while long bunching onions need trenches 15 cm deep. As the seedlings grow the trenches are gradually filled in. As the long bunching types grow, gradually mound up the soil to a height of 30 cm above ground level to blanch the stems. Short bunching onions can also be propagated by dividing existing clumps and do not need to have the soil mounded up around the stems.

Bunching onions can be harvested all year round. If they are being grown for spring onions then they can be harvested after only two months; short bunching types take about four months while long bunching onions can take eight months.

Use Both the leaves and stems of bunching onions are eaten. They have a mild, sweet, onion flavour early in the season but the flavour strengthens as the plant reaches maturity. The stem contains some vitamin C and small amounts of carotene, potassium and dietary fibre. In China and Japan, the white and green stems are commonly used in stir-fries because they cook quickly. Overcooking can make them bitter. The Vietnamese add leaves to soups, and both leaves and stems to beef stir-fry. In other Asian cultures the leaves are used as a garnish (often cut into little brushes) and are also added for their flavour and deep green colour to soups, noodle dishes and salads. In Western cooking, bunching onions are mainly used like spring onions to supply young growth for salads, stews and soups. They are particularly good in potato soup in winter when other onions are harder to get, or combined with cheese and bacon in omelettes and quiches.

Allium sativum Alliaceae

garlic

chyet-thon-phew (Bu); suen tau, taai suan (ChC); suan, hu suan (ChM); bawang putih (In); nin-niku (Ja); ktim saa (Kh); ka thiem (La); bawang putih (Ma); krathiem (Th); toi (Vi)

The earliest records of garlic come from Egyptian cemeteries, where clay models of the bulb have been dated back to 3750 BC. Garlic was in common use in Ancient China where it is mentioned in the *Calender of the Hsia,* parts of which date back to 2000 BC. It is now widely grown throughout Asia and is an essential part of most Asian cuisines.

Description Garlic is a flat-leafed perennial that is usually grown as an annual. Plants grow to about 40 cm and in some cultivars in late summer, a rounded stalk appears from the centre of the plant. This stalk bears a rounded flower head enclosed in a papery spathe. The spathe splits to reveal a cluster of bulbils and occasional pinkish-white flowers.

Cultivation Garlic can be grown by dividing the familiar bulb and planting the individual cloves from autumn to early spring, or by planting the bulbils found in the flower head of some cultivars. It usually takes two years for a mature bulb with cloves to grow from a bulbil. Plant cloves about 2 cm below the surface of the soil and space them 10 cm apart in rows 40 cm apart. Garlic does best in light soils with good drainage, although heavier soils are all right if cloves are planted into raised ridges to improve the drainage.

Enrich the soil with well-rotted manure or fish meal before planting, and top-dress with blood and bone during winter and early spring. Mulch around the plants and water regularly while the bulbs are growing. Stop watering as soon as the tops begin to turn brown, as the bulbs are then nearly ready, and too much water will cause the bulbs to split and rot. Harvest garlic about eight months after planting. Some of the leaves will be brown, and flower stems (if present) starting to go soft. Harvest by digging up the whole plant with a fork and shaking gently to remove excess dirt. Hang in bunches or spread on racks to dry for two or three weeks in a dry, airy position out of direct light.

In China, garlic is sometimes sprouted to provide nutritious, tasty greens in winter. To do this, plant cloves about 2 cm apart. When the green leaves are about 20 cm high cut them back to 1 cm above the ground and use the green leaves. Cloves will reshoot another two or three times before they are exhausted. Also in China, garlic is grown as green garlic shoots, where the whole plant is harvested after only three to four months' growth. At this stage the bulbs are known as 'rounds' and have not formed cloves. Sometimes green garlic is blanched first by mounding dirt around each plant.

Like shallots, most garlic does not do well in tropical regions. However, cultivars like 'Glenlarge' are not dependent on day length so can be grown in regions with short days. Alternatively, those living in the tropics can grow garlic sprouts or green garlic.

Use Garlic has numerous culinary and medicinal properties. It is also a useful companion plant as it has the ability to repel both airborne and soil-borne pests. In Thailand, garlic is an essential part of many dishes. It is often crushed and pounded and made into a seasoning paste. Alternatively it is deep-fried, whole or sliced, until crisp and used to garnish soup and noodle dishes. Garlic is also an important component of many stir-fries. In Vietnam, garlic is essential to most savoury dishes. Often it is added to the cooking oil and fried before adding any other ingredients. In China, garlic is eaten as sprouts, green garlic and garlic cloves. Freshly sprouted garlic leaves are added to salads and stir-fries. Garlic flower stems are also eaten and regarded as a delicacy. These are harvested while the stems are green and before the flower head opens. They are used fresh in stir-fries and soups or can be dried for winter use. The Vietnamese use garlic medicinally to treat heart disease, high blood pressure and as part of a compress for skin eruptions like acne and boils.

Allium tuberosum Alliaceae

garlic chives, Chinese chives, Chinese leeks, oriental garlic, flowering leek

gau tsoi, kau tsoi (ChC); kiu, jiu kai (ChM); kucai (In); nira (Ja); kuu chaay (Kh); phak pen (La); kucai, bawang kucai (Ma); bai kuchai, dok kuichai, ton kui chai (Th); he (Vi)

Garlic chives have been used for centuries in China and Japan. In the Chinese *Book of Poems*, dating from at least 500 BC, *kiu* is mentioned as being offered in sacrifice with lamb. It is likely that *kiu* was regarded as a precious or holy vegetable at that time. Garlic chives are also listed in a dictionary of the Han period (206 BC–AD 220), and records exist of their cultivation in Japan as early as AD 928. They were introduced to Australia by Asian immigrants early in the 20th century, and are now grown commercially for the green leaves, blanched leaves and flower buds with stems in New South Wales, Northern Territory, Tasmania and Victoria.

Description Perennial plants that live for many years, garlic chives grow from large spreading rhizomes with green strap-like leaves that grow to a height of 40 cm. The umbels of flowers that grow on hollow stalks reach 50 cm and are white, starlike and sweetly scented. There are leafy and flowering cultivars, but the best ones to grow (and those most widely available) can be used for both.

Cultivation Garlic chives will grow in most climates, producing leafy growth for most of the year and flowers in summer.

In warmer areas they will not die back. They grow best at daytime maximums of 18°–24°C. If temperatures are higher then the leaves are not as tender, but lower temperatures will slow growth. Garlic chives grow in any soil but do best in light, sandy soils that are high in organic matter. They are not fussy about whether the soil is acid or alkaline. To grow blanched leaves, cover plants with black plastic, straw or earth so that the leaves are grown in the dark and become soft and yellow. Alternate blanched harvests with green harvests to give the plants time to recover. In good conditions up to eight harvests a year may be possible. Alternatively pick a few leaves from a clump any time they are needed.

Propagate from seed or by dividing clumps. Sow seed at any time, but garlic chives will germinate faster at soil temperatures of about 20°C. Seed needs to be fairly fresh (less than a year old) and should be black and shiny. Plant in clumps of about 10 plants, with 20 cm between clumps. Don't overwater, especially blanched leaves, as they may rot. Established clumps may need to have earth mounded up around them, or to be dug and replanted every few years as the soil becomes depleted, and the rhizomes gradually work their way out of the soil. In warmer regions, garlic chives can self-sow prolifically, so remove the flower heads before they set seed.

Leaves are harvested by cutting them just below the soil surface, as much of the flavour is in the base of the leaf. To harvest flower buds for use, cut at the base of the stem before the bud opens.

Use Garlic chives are used as both a herb and a vegetable, and are mostly lightly cooked rather than eaten raw, because of their strong flavour. Leaves, flower stems and flowers are all eaten and have a distinct garlic-onion flavour, while blanched leaves have a more subtle garlic flavour. They are often added to noodle dishes with bean curd, spring rolls, dumplings, omelettes and mushrooms. They are also dressed with salt and sesame oil and served as a salad. In Vietnam, leaves are eaten fresh in rice paper rolls and added to a range of different soups. Garlic chives are high in vitamins A and C as well as iron and calcium. Blanched leaves are more of a delicacy and need to be used very fresh, but they are used in much the same ways as the green leaves. Flower stems maintain their green colour when cooked. They are delicious stir-fried with bean sprouts or added to salads. The Javanese deep-fry small bunches in batter, while the Chinese stir-fry them as a side dish with beef or bean curd. Medicinally, the leaves are ground and the juice drunk to ease bronchial problems, and a paste made from the leaves and roots is used to ease the pain from toothache.

Alpinia galanga   Zingiberaceae

galangal, greater galangal, Thai ginger, galingale

pa de gaw gyi (Bu); lam kieu (ChH); gao liang jiang (ChM); laos (In); romdeng (Kh); kha ta deng (La); lengkuas (Ma); kha (Th); rieng (Vi)

This member of the ginger family comes originally from the Malay Peninsula, and is now cultivated in most tropical regions of South-East Asia. It was imported into Europe along Mesopotamian trade routes since at least the 12th century, when it was known as galingale and esteemed as an aphrodisiac. One writer assures us that galangal is "efficacious for all ailments of elephants".

Description A perennial plant, galangal grows from thick rhizomes that are usually 10 – 12 cm long and about 3 cm wide. It grows as a dense clump with long, narrow, delightfully scented leaves to nearly 2 m. The flower head can be 20 cm long and is made up of numerous short branches, each with three to five creamy-white flowers. Flowers are followed by red, spherical fruit.

Cultivation Galangal grows well in the tropics in shady positions. Propagate by dividing rhizomes and replanting into a fertile, humus-rich, well-drained soil. Plant rhizomes just below the soil surface about 60 cm apart. In tropical regions it can be grown as a useful screen or hedge. In cooler regions, grow it in a sheltered, warm but shaded corner or in a pot in a similar position. In very cold climates,

galangal can only be grown in a heated greenhouse.

Use Rhizomes, young shoots and leaves are all eaten. Young, new shoots are pale pink, while older ones are pale-brown. Young rhizomes and shoots are more tender and have more flavour than older ones. The flavour is pungent and spicy (quite different from ginger). Rhizomes are usually cooked before eating. Slices or chunks are added to a range of dishes and removed before serving. Alternatively, they can be sliced and cut into very small

pieces before being pounded into a paste that is added to curries and side dishes. One dish that uses galangal paste is the popular Thai soup made from chicken, galangal and coconut milk; in this the galangal is the predominant flavour. In Indonesia, galangal is often used in preference to ginger. It is possible to buy dried and pickled galangal roots in Asian groceries but the flavour is not the same as fresh rhizomes. Shoots, flower buds and flowers can also be cooked (usually steamed) and eaten, and the leaves are used to wrap fish. Flower buds and flowers are sometimes dipped in batter and cooked. Galangal root, sliced and made into a tea that is sweetened and drunk cold, is used in several Asian countries to soothe stomach-aches and relieve nausea.

Amaranthus tricolor   Amaranthaceae

amaranth, Chinese spinach, edible amaranth, leaf amaranth

in tsoi, yin choi (ChC); heng-chai (ChH); xian cai (ChM); bayam (In); hi-yu-na, Java hohrensoj (Ja); phti (Kh); phak houm (La); bayam (Ma); kulitis (Ph); phak khom (Th); rau den (Vi)

Amaranth has been cultivated for at least 8000 years. The Mayans of South and Central America grew it, as did the Aztecs, who used it in religious ceremonies. It has been grown in southern China for centuries. Today *Amaranthus* species are grown throughout the tropics for both their seeds and leaves.

Description The species grown for seed production is different to the one grown for its leaf. Leaf amaranth, *A. tricolor* is the plant grown and most used in Asia. It is an annual that grows to over 1 m with fleshy thick stems. Leaf shape is very variable but they are usually ovate and green or green and purple in colour. The flowers are generally green or red and occur in terminal spikes. There are cultivars of this plant that are grown specifically for their leaf colour, which adds striking foliage colour to the garden bed. If a green variety is grown next to a red variety, then the plants will cross-pollinate and the next generation will be a mixture of leaf colours.

Cultivation In temperate regions, grow amaranth from seeds sown into the garden in spring. Ideal soil temperatures are about 20°C when seed will germinate in about four days. Seed will still germinate at lower temperatures but will take longer. It can be sown all year round in the tropics but for succulent leaf growth make sure it gets plenty of water during dry periods. Thin to about 15 cm between plants in all directions. Edible amaranth needs a reasonably well-composted soil high in nutrients, but apart from this is not fussy and can be grown in most soils. It also likes full, hot sun. Begin to harvest the leaves as soon as plants have enough leaves to make it possible. Keep harvesting until flowers appear; by this time leaves will no longer be tender enough to eat. Water stress, short days and sometimes transplant shock may all make amaranth begin to flower and go to seed. Plants will self-sow readily and may become weedy, so before seed is set, pull the whole plant out and add to the compost or feed to poultry or stock. Let one plant go to seed to provide seed for the following year.

Use Edible amaranth leaves have a sweet but tangy flavour. They are high in vita-

min C, carotene, calcium, folic acid, iron and protein. They contain twice as much iron as ordinary spinach and also some vitamin A and potassium. The whole plant (except the roots) is eaten when very young and fresh leaves are occasionally added to salads. As amaranth leaves are fairly high in both nitrates and oxalic acid it is important not to eat them fresh too often. Mostly, the leaves are boiled and the water discarded before eating. Only ever cook for two or three minutes. In Japan and China, cooked leaves are added to salads, soups and stir-fries as well as being served as a side dish. Leaves combine well with other vegetables, especially garlic and ginger. Where an Asian recipe calls for spinach it is usually amaranth that is meant. Amaranth stems are also eaten, usually peeled first and then steamed, and the leaves and stems can be pickled in salt.

Anethum graveolens Apiaceae

dill

adas manis (In); phak xi, phak si (La); pak chee lao (Th); thi la (Vi)

Dill comes originally from South-West Asia but is now naturalised in many parts of Europe and northern USA.

Description Dill is a tall annual herb that grows to over 1 m. The single stem grows from a strong taproot. It produces many feathery blue-green branches and is topped in summer by a cluster of umbels made up of small yellow flowers. The flowers are followed by flat, oval brown seeds which will self-sow readily if left on the plant.

Cultivation Grow dill from seed sown where the plants are to grow, as seedlings do not transplant well. Sow seed in spring and summer in temperate regions and autumn in the tropics. Just cover seed with soil and thin to about 30 cm between plants. In Asia, dill is often sown densely and whole leafy plants harvested when they are only about 15 cm high. In warm weather, the plants will mature in about seven weeks, so successive plantings will be needed to maintain a supply of fresh foliage. Dill grows well in full sun in rich, fertile soil with lots of organic matter. Keep well watered during dry weather. As plants self-sow readily, allow a few plants to go to seed to ensure a crop for the following year. Seed heads should be harvested just as the seed starts to turn brown. Dry seed on paper in a cool, shady,

airy position. Store in an airtight container out of direct light. Dill is a good companion plant for Chinese brassicas as it helps to repel cabbage moth.

Use Both the leaves and seeds are used for culinary and medicinal purposes. The seeds aid digestion by easing stomachaches that are caused by wind, and dill water is often given to children to relieve colic. The leaves have a distinct, pleasant hard-to-describe flavour. They are best used fresh, but can be frozen for later use. The Thais, Vietnamese and Laotians all use both the leaves and seeds. Vietnamese people usually use dill leaves as a garnish or salad herb, while in Laos they are cooked as a vegetable. Add leaves to fresh cucumber and yoghurt as a side dish and sprinkle chopped leaves over any dish containing lamb, just before serving.

Apium graveolens   Apiaceae

Chinese celery, Asian celery, leaf celery, cutting celery, soup celery

k'an tsoi, kintsai, kun choi, hon cun (ChC); kun cai (ChH); qing cai (ChM); seri-na (Ja); selderi (In); khinchhay (Kh); phak sen leu ri (La); selderi, daun sop (Ma); kinchay (Ph); ceun chai, phak chi lom, khen chaai (Th); can (Vi)

Celery is probably native to both northern Asia and Europe and was certainly used in Egyptian, Roman and Greek cultures. Celery is mentioned in Chinese literature as early as the 5th century AD when it was regarded as an important medicinal plant. Chinese celery is derived from the northern Asian form. In Asian markets, Chinese celery is usually sold with other herbs like coriander, rather than with vegetables.

Description Chinese celery is a straggly, slender, biennial plant that reaches only about 40 cm in height. It is a much lower-growing plant with shorter and less succulent stems than ordinary celery. Chinese celery has furrowed, hollow stems, dissected, bright green leaves and tiny white flowers. There are several different cultivars, and the leaf and stem colour can vary from white through creamy yellow to dark green.

23

Cultivation Sow the seed directly into the soil in spring in temperate regions. In tropical regions it is a winter crop and should be sown in autumn. If seed is sown too early in spring, then the cold will cause the plants to bolt to seed, lessening the harvest time. Germination can take up to 20 days even at ideal soil temperatures of 21°C. Thin plants to about 15 cm between each seedling. Chinese celery likes a relatively rich, well-drained soil and prefers full sun, although it will tolerate some shade. In tropical and subtropical regions Chinese celery grows best in the shade. Water well during dry weather as plants that have been allowed to dry out will have tough stems. Feed occasionally with seaweed fertiliser to promote

green growth. Pick the leaves and young stems as soon as plants are large enough to withstand harvest, and continue to harvest right through summer into autumn. Pick one stem at a time or harvest the whole plant by cutting a few centimetres above the ground and allowing the plant to regrow. Chinese celery can be grown as part of a border to a vegetable garden. It can also be grown in a flower garden to provide dense, bright green foliage that acts as a foil to the flowers.

Use Chinese celery is grown more for its leaves than its stems, although the stems can also be used. Its flavour is much stronger than ordinary celery. Add a few leaves or finely chopped stems to salads, soups, stews, stir-fried rice and noodles. Often the leaves and stems are stir-fried first. Remember that this herb is strongly flavoured so don't use too much. Stems can be stir-fried on their own, with a little soy sauce and sesame seeds, or add bean sprouts and other vegetables for an interesting vegetable stir-fry. Celery leaves also make an excellent garnish. Celery seeds are sometimes used as a spice.

Arctium lappa   Asteraceae

burdock, beggar's buttons, cockly, edible burdock, flapper-bags, gobo, great burdock, harlock, hurr-burrs

ngao pong (ChC); niu pang, dong yang luo bo (ChM); gobo (Ja)

Burdock is native to most of Europe and temperate regions of China. It was probably introduced to Japan from China where it has been used and valued for its medicinal properties for centuries. It is grown commercially in Japan, where it is an important food crop, and it has been grown commercially (though on a small scale) in New South Wales, Tasmania, Victoria and Western Australia.

Description Burdock is a tall-growing biennial or short-lived perennial that starts as a clump of very large, grey-green wavy-edged leaves. The leaves and stem are covered with fine hairs and the underside of the leaf is much paler in colour. In the second year a tall branched flower stalk to 2 m grows from the centre of this clump. Flowers are small, numerous, purple or white and are followed by spiky seedpods. Burdock roots are long and slender and resemble parsnips although they can be more than a metre long. The skin is brown and the flesh white.

There are several different cultivars of burdock. They vary mainly in their root length and thickness. The Japanese use cultivars known as 'Takinogawa' (long slender roots), 'Oura', 'Hagi' and 'Echizen Shiroguki'.

Cultivation Burdock does well in a temperate climate but also likes warm and humid regions. In cold frosty areas, leaves will die back completely but roots will survive air temperatures as low as -20°C. They then reshoot in spring. Sow seed in spring or autumn. Burdock is a winter crop in Darwin.

Burdock grows best in a deep, sandy-loam soil that has been deeply dug. This is necessary for long, strong root development. Plants need full sun and good drainage and do best in soils that have a pH of 6.5 – 7.5. Burdock does not grow well in acid soils. Since this root vegetable is prone to nematode attack, plant tagetes marigolds, oats or rape in the ground where burdock is to be grown and then dig them into soil before planting. Don't add high-nitrogen fertilisers (like fresh manures) as this will cause forking of the roots. Conversely, high phosphorous fertilisers will encourage strong root growth.

Sow seed directly into well-prepared soil to a depth of 1.5 cm when soil temperatures are at least 10°C. The highest germination rates are seen at soil temperatures between 20° – 25°C. In very warm regions, plant seed in early spring as higher temperatures will inhibit seed germination. Seed germinates more readily if it is

soaked for about 12 hours first, or scarified on fine sand paper. Even so it may take up to two weeks to germinate.

Thin plants to a spacing of about 20 cm in all directions. This close spacing encourages long straight roots. Once plants are growing well don't water too often but always give a good soaking; this will force the roots to search more deeply for water. Keep weed-free when young. Mulching helps to suppress weeds and reduce watering.

Roots can be harvested after about three to five months from seed sown in spring, or five to eight months from seed sown in autumn. Young leaves and immature roots can be harvested in spring after only a few weeks growth, but burdock is usually grown for its mature roots. These are harvested in summer and autumn and should be about 25 mm in diameter and over 60 cm long. To harvest, dig deeply with a garden fork and gently tug on the tops until the whole plant comes free. Roots that are left for too long become woody and tough, and the flavour of the root is not as good once plants have flowered. It is a good idea to remove the flowers anyway to stop the plant from setting seed, as the prickly seed pods are a nuisance and the whole plant has the potential to become a problem weed.

Use Fresh burdock root is sweetly pungent, similar to Jerusalem artichokes. It also has a delightful texture. Young roots are peeled and eaten fresh (often with a little salt). Mature roots are peeled, soaked in water for about an hour and then boiled, or julienned and added to stir-fries, or deep-fried or simply added to soups and stews. They are also pickled, made into a paste, drunk as a tea and even made into a soft drink. *Kimpera*, which is a popular dish in Japan, is made from slices of burdock root fried in a sweet sauce made from sugar, soy and sesame. Young leaves and shoots can be eaten, cooked as a vegetable. If thinning out plants try cooking the leaves with the tiny root attached as a vegetable on its own. Medicinally, burdock has been used as a diuretic and to relieve arthritic pain. It is also supposed to be an aphrodisiac. Burdock roots are high in fibre and vitamin B but low in calories. They also contain starch, potash, inulin, resin and several substances that appear to have antibiotic properties.

Bambusa spp., *Dendrocalamus* spp., and *Phyllostachys* spp. Poaceae

bamboo shoots

wah-bho-hmyit (Bu); sun (ChC); soon (ChH); zhu sun (ChM); rebung (In); takenoko (Ja); tumpaeng (Kh); no mai (La); buloh betong, rebung (Ma); labong (Ph); no mai (Th); mang (Vi)

There are probably as many as 1200 species of bamboo all over the world, in climates varying from temperate to tropical, and many of these are useful to humans. In Asian countries, bamboo is used for baskets, boats, buildings and bridges, fences, furniture and fishing rods as well as walking-sticks and weapons. It is hardly surprising that it is also eaten. Bamboos for edible bamboo shoots are grown commercially in Queensland and Northern Territory.

Description Shoots from *B.oldhamii, B. vulgaris, D. asper, D. brandisii, D. giganteus, D. latiflorus, P. angusta, P. aurea, P. dulcis, P.nigra, P. nuda* and *P. suphurea* var. *viridis*, along with many others too numerous to mention here, can all be eaten. Bamboo grows as short or long stems, known as culms, from spreading underground rootstock. *Bambusa* and *Dendrocalamus* species are all clumping forms that do not spread rapidly, while *Phyllostachys* species are all spreading forms, although they spread very slowly in cool climates. Leaves are usually green and narrow lanceolate in shape. Bamboo flowers are typically grasslike, and culms with flowers often die back. Some bamboos only flower every 100 years or more.

Cultivation Grow new plants by dividing old ones or by taking cuttings from the underground rhizomes. These cuttings should be about 20 cm long and planted horizontally 15 cm deep. Bamboo likes a humus-rich soil with a lot of added manure and slightly damp conditions. *Dendrocalamus* species grow best in tropical regions and cannot tolerate air temperatures below 10°C. *Bambusa* species are more cold tolerant and will cope with temperatures just below freezing, while *Phyllostachys* species will tolerate even lower temperatures but not for prolonged periods. Most bamboos like full sun.

Cultivating bamboo to harvest its edible shoots is regarded as a highly specialised art in Japan, where a crop can take from three to seven years from first

Freshly picked bamboo shoots (photograph by H.F. Chin)

Culms and leaves of *B. oldhamii*

become bitter. When the tips just appear from this mound scrape away the mud and manure and cut off the shoot at ground level with a sharp knife. This shoot does not grow again. Use fresh bamboo shoots as soon as possible after harvest to stop them from becoming bitter.

Use After harvest, wash the shoots with the husk still on, then remove about three layers of the husk and the hard base. Most bamboo shoots are poisonous when raw because they contain hydrocyanic acid. Boiling the shoots destroys the hydrocyanic acid; this generally takes about 30 minutes. Sprinkle salt over the boiled pieces as they are removed from the water. If they are still bitter then boil again. Freshly cooked bamboo shoots are crisp. They can be eaten as a vegetable or added to stir-fries, salads and soups. Bamboo shoots are also often pickled in vinegar or salt.

planting to first harvest. Shoots should be harvested before they actually emerge from the ground. To achieve this, mound up around each just-emerged shoot with manure and mud to about 20 cm so that the new shoots are completely covered. If they are left exposed to the sun then they

Basella alba and *B. alba* 'Rubra'   Basellaceae

basella, Malabar spinach, Ceylon spinach, climbing spinach, Indian spinach, Surinam spinach, country spinach, vine spinach, slippery vegetable

shaan tsoi, san choi, lok kwai, hung tang tsoi (ChC); luo kui, mu er cai, lu luo kui, zi luo kui, ruan jian cai, yan zhi dou (ChM); gandola (In); tsuru-murasaki (Ja); phakkang (La); remayung, gendola (Ma); alogbati (Ph); pak prang (Th); mong toi (Vi)

This leafy vegetable is grown throughout tropical regions of Asia and is probably native to India and China. In China, the purple-red dye, which comes from the fleshy berries when squeezed, was used by government officials to stamp documents.

28

Description There are two main varieties of basella, one with fleshy green stems and leaves and white flowers (*B. alba*), the other with red-purple stems and purple-green leaves with pink flowers (*B. alba* 'Rubra'). They are both short-lived perennials with large oval leaves and a twisting climbing growth habit. The flowers grow in spikes from the leaf axils.

Cultivation Grow basella from cuttings or seed. Seed remains viable for up to five years. Ideal germination temperatures for the soil are 18° – 21°C and seed will germinate more readily if they are soaked in water first. In temperate regions, start basella inside in individual pots and transplant outside when the last chance of frost is over because plants are very frost-tender. In warmer regions plant directly into soil that has been enriched with plenty of manure. Plant seed 2 cm deep at the base of a trellis about 1.5 m high. Alternatively, plant at the base of a tripod of similar height. Basella also grows well in hanging baskets. It will not grow vigorously until the weather really warms up. In regions with very hot, dry summers, basella will need plenty of water and may need to be shaded during hot afternoons. Start harvesting about two months after sowing. Cut the tips off the branches to encourage new bushy growth.

Use Stems, young shoots and leaves are all eaten. They make a good substitute for spinach in any recipe, retaining their bright green colour. The red form turns green when cooked. Basella is delicious in stir-fries as long as it is not overcooked as it will then become slimy and mucilaginous. Leaves are also added to soups and stews where the mucilaginous qualities can be used for thickening. A delicious soup can be made by adding basella leaves, water, bean curd and hard boiled eggs to freshly fried ginger. In China this is known as "slippery soup". Fresh leaves are added to salads. Basella is high in vitamins A and C and a good source of iron and calcium as well as other minerals. It also has mild laxative properties. The berries produce a red dye that can be used to colour desserts such as jelly and pastry.

Basella alba

Benincasa hispida   Cucurbitaceae

wax gourd, white gourd, winter gourd, Chinese zucchini, Chinese preserving melon, Chinese squash, ash gourd, ash pumpkin

tung kwa (ChC); dong gua (ChM); tohgan (Ja); kundur bulat (Ma); fak (Th)

This gourd is grown in many tropical countries including the Caribbean, China, India, Indonesia, Malaysia and the Philippines. In some regions it is seen growing over the roofs of houses, and in India, there are several superstitions attached to this fruit so that it is unlikely to be stolen. In Australia, wax gourds are grown commercially in New South Wales, Northern Territory and Queensland.

Description   There are a variety of cultivars — some are better harvested immature, others when they are mature. This is a very vigorous climbing plant with angled, hairy stems and very large, lobed, dark green leaves. Male and female flowers are large and yellow while the fruit is more rounded than oblong with a waxy bloom when mature. Wax gourds are often confused with fuzzy gourds (see page 00), to which they are closely related. Part of the confusion stems from the fact that young wax gourds are often covered with fine hairs, but these disappear as the gourd matures.

Cultivation   Wax gourds need a long growing season, often more than five months, to reach maturity. They do best in tropical regions when daytime maximums are 24° – 32 °C. Plant into well-drained soil that has been well manured and make sure there is plenty of space. They are best grown on the ground rather than trellised so that the fruits can be allowed to grow to their full size without support. Wax gourds do best in soil with a pH of about 6.5.

In cooler regions, to extend the growing season, germinate seed on wet paper, using a heated propagator with bottom heat of about 28°C. Seed should sprout in three to five days. Plant into individual pots and try to keep the minimum air temperature above 10°C. Transplant into the garden once the seedlings are about 18 cm tall. Leave about 70 cm between plants, and if planting rows, 1.5 m between rows.

If planting directly into the soil, place four or five seeds in each position at the above spacings and thin to the healthiest

plant once they are growing vigorously. Plants grown on trellises can be more closely spaced but the fruit will need to be supported. Nip out the growing tips after about three weeks, to leave four lateral shoots. Flowering should start after two months, and if fruit is not setting because it is too cold, try hand pollinating. Fertilise every two weeks with a handful of compost and chicken manure, but stop once the fruit starts to set. Young wax gourds can be picked when they are three to four weeks old and the optimum size is about 1.5 kg. Gourds can reach 20 kg, but once they are as big as this they can only be used to make soups or stews. If gourds are sitting on the ground, place a handful of straw underneath to stop rot and keep the gourds clean.

Wax gourds are relatively drought tolerant, although if they are too water stressed then the gourds may well be woody. In some Thai villages wax gourds are intercropped with maize.

Use Young gourds can be eaten as a vegetable, cooked in the same way as marrows and zucchini, and the flavour is that of a slightly sweet zucchini. They are also delicious in stir-fries. Older gourds are usually added to soups and are an essential ingredient of the Chinese 'Winter melon pond soup'. Gourd flesh is also pickled and made into sweet preserves similar in texture to Turkish delight. The leaves, young growing tips, flower buds and seeds are also eaten. The seeds have an interesting, slightly bitter flavour and are usually roasted first. Flower buds and growing tips are cooked as a vegetable, added to stir-fries or chopped and sprinkled over a salad. The hollowed-out end of the gourd can be used as a soup bowl. Mature wax gourds with a good white waxy coat can be stored for as long as one year, making them a valuable crop when food is scarce.

Benincasa hispida var. *chieh-gua*   Cucurbitaceae

fuzzy gourd, hairy gourd, hairy cucumber, fuzzy melon, jointed gourd, Chinese squash, moqua

mo kwa (ChC); mao gua, jie gua (ChM); kundur panjang (Ma)

Widely distributed through tropical regions of the world, this melon probably comes originally from southern China. It is grown commercially in New South Wales, Northern Territory and Queensland.

Description This annual climbing vine has coarse, hairy stems with trailing tendrils. The leaves are lobed and male and female flowers occur on different parts of the plant, the male flowers having long

stems and the female flowers comparatively short stems. Flowers are yellow. The flesh can be yellow or white. There are a variety of cultivars that vary in size and shape but they are usually plump and elongated, longer than wide and covered with fine hairs. This gourd is usually harvested immature and adult fruit have little or no waxy bloom.

Cultivation Fuzzy gourds are grown in exactly the same way as wax gourds (see page 30) and like the same conditions. The exception is that fuzzy gourds lend themselves more to growth on a trellis, because they are usually harvested young.

Young fuzzy gourds can be picked as early as one week after fruit-set, but the optimum time is when they are three to four weeks old, about 12 cm long and still covered by fine hairs.

Use Young fruit can be eaten raw but are more usually cooked. Before cutting, always remove the fine hairs on the outside of the fruit by rubbing with paper and then washing in cold water. Use in the same way as wax gourds, but these gourds are particularly good stuffed. In China, they are stuffed with shrimp and pork mixed with vegetables. Fuzzy gourds have a delicious flavour, a bit stronger and more distinctive than some of the better known squashes. If the fruit is stored for too long the flavour changes and becomes more acidic and less palatable. Fruits are high in vitamin C and low in fat.

Bixa orellana Bixaceae

lipstick tree, annatto, achiote

kesumba (In); jarak belanda, kesumba (Ma); atsuete (Ph); kam tai (Th); hat dieu mau (seed) (Vi)

This decorative tree comes originally from tropical central and southern America, but was introduced to the Philippines by the Spanish. It has spread from there to other Asian countries.

Description A small tree or large bush, lipstick tree can grow as tall as 7 m but it is usually smaller. Leaves are dark green and broadly ovate, while flowers that appear in summer are bright pink and very attractive to bees. Flowers are followed by furry, bright red seedpods that turn brown when ripe and split to reveal 40-50 bright red seeds.

Cultivation This tropical tree is grown from seed or from cuttings that are placed in sand or good seed raising mix. In temperate regions these seeds or cuttings will need to be placed in a heated propagator. Plants grown from cuttings tend to flower at a younger age than those grown from seed. Lipstick trees like a sunny position and well-drained soils that are high in organic matter. Water well during dry weather. These trees can be grown in temperate regions but they need a warm, protected corner that is frost-free. Trees will sometimes reshoot after mild frosts. They can be grown as a hedge (space plants about 1 m apart) and benefit from regular cutting and shaping.

Use Seeds are used as a food colouring or dye in the Philippines. Fry the seeds in oil so that it takes on the red colour. Use this oil to cook paella and other rice dishes. Alternatively, soak the seeds in water and use this water to cook. In China, the seeds are used to colour meat such as pork. In Central America, the spice, annatto, is made from the seeds.

Boesenbergia rotunda   Zingiberaceae
syn. *B. pandurata*

Chinese keys, lesser galangal

suo shi (ChM); kunci, temu kunci (In); kcheay (Kh); temu kunci (Ma); krachai (Th)

This plant grows throughout South-East Asia although it probably came originally from Indonesia where it is still found growing wild in Java.

Description   Chinese keys is a tropical plant that grows to about 60 cm with long, green, oblong leaves to about 30 cm. In cold regions leaves will die back in winter. Flowers are pink or white and grow in spikes. The roots grow in clusters of yellow-brown finger-like protrusions that are long and slender and taper to a point. They are hot, peppery, aromatic and spicy in scent and flavour.

Cultivation   Although this is a tropical plant it can be grown in temperate regions in a pot in a warm sheltered position, and moved inside or into a heated greenhouse in winter. Propagate new plants from pieces of root with one or two buds, planted to a depth of about 5 cm, in spring. They like a fertile, open, loamy soil that is well drained because they do not like to be waterlogged. The rhizome will grow more quickly if the planting area is covered in clear plastic to maintain warmth and humidity. This is removed once shoots appear. In regions with dry, hot summers, frequent misting with water is

essential. Plants need a warm, shady position and regular watering. Chinese keys grows wild in regions with more than 1000 mm of rainfall a year. In the tropics plants need little attention; simply plant rhizomes in spring or autumn, in a shady position, and harvest the roots the following autumn.

Use In Thailand, these roots are peeled and eaten raw in salads, added to soup and fish curry, and sometimes pickled. The roots are also used in some soups in Indonesia and Cambodia and young leaves and shoots are eaten too. The

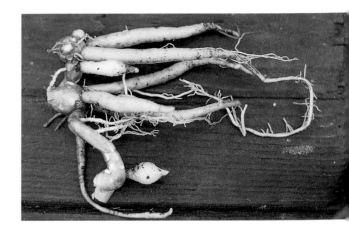

Chinese are more likely to use this root medicinally than in cooking. They use it to treat colic and diarrhoea.

Brassica juncea Brassicaceae

Chinese mustard, mustard greens, brown mustard, Indian mustard, leaf mustard, mustard cabbage

kaai tsoi, gai choy, kai-choi (ChC); tua-chia (ChH); jie cai, gai cai (ChM); cai sin (In); karashina, takana (Ja); spey choeung tie (Kh); phak kat khieo (La); sawi sawi (Ma); phak kwang tung khiao (Th); cai be xanh (Vi)

This mustard is extensively cultivated in China, Africa and Eastern Europe. It probably comes originally from Asia and has been cultivated there for centuries.

Description Chinese mustard grows to over 1 m with elliptic, deeply divided, dark green leaves, the end segment of which is ovate. These leaves taper towards the stem and have a strong mustard flavour. The flowers are pale yellow and four-petalled in terminal racemes. They are followed by long, narrow seedpods containing reddish-brown seed. There are a large number of cultivars that vary in leaf shape and size. Two cultivars sold in Singapore markets are known as 'Wrapped Heart Mustard' and 'Bamboo Mustard' but there are many others. Broad-leafed mustard (*Brassica juncea* var. *rugosa*) is similar to Chinese mustard except that the leaves are larger and more crinkled.

Cultivation Production is similar to Chinese cabbage (see page 43). Chinese mustard is a cool season crop that is mainly planted in spring and autumn; however, it is fairly cold-sensitive and most varieties won't survive a heavy frost. Chinese mustard does best in fertile, well-drained, sandy-loam soils with a pH of 5.5 – 6.8. This plant is more tolerant of poor soils and acidity than most of the other brassicas.

Sow seed into punnets and transplant when the seedlings are about three weeks old, spacing plants about 30 cm apart.

Alternatively, sow direct into shallow trenches and thin to about 30 cm between plants. In commercial crops, the harvest of whole plants takes place about 45 days after transplanting. In the home garden, outside leaves can be harvested, leaving the rest of the plant to continue growing. Harvest seeds in autumn. Pick the pods while they are still just green and hang upside down to dry in a warm, airy position. Tie paper bags over the seedheads to stop the seed from dropping on the floor when the pods dry out and split.

Use This leafy mustard is mainly grown to produce fresh, green mustard leaves used in salads. The flavour is hot and tangy. In Vietnam, leaves are also added to soups, combined with chicken and ginger in stir-fries and steamed or boiled as a vegetable. In northern China and Korea, the leaves and stems are often pickled or salted and served as a side dish. Chinese mustard is high in vitamins A, B and C as well as iron and potassium. Some cultivars are grown for their stems which are peeled and pickled. The seed is very aromatic and is used in coarse continental mustards. In many Asian cuisines, the aromatic seed is fried gently until it starts to pop and then added to vegetable dishes. Seeds are also ground and added to pastes, pickles and chutneys. This mustard seed is an important ingredient in both Malaysia and Singapore. Chinese mustard is a useful green manure crop, adding nutrients to the soil and suppressing some root diseases.

Brassica oleracea Alboglabra Group Brassicaceae
syn. *B. oleracea* var. *alboglabra,*

Chinese broccoli, Chinese kale, white flowering broccoli

kaai laan tsoi, gai lum, kailan (ChC); gai lan, jie lan (ChM); kol (In); khatna (Kh); phak khana (La); kai lan (Ma); phak khana (Th); cai ro (Vi)

Chinese broccoli is closely related to European broccoli. It may have been introduced to China from Portugal in the mid 1500s, or may have come originally from southern China. It is grown commercially in New South Wales, Northern Territory, Queensland, Western Australia and Victoria.

Description Chinese broccoli is a fast-growing brassica with a single fleshy stem and dark green, rounded leaves on long stems. The leaves are usually darker green than those of Chinese flowering cabbage (see page 40). Plants will start to flower when about 10 leaves are present. Flowers are white. A perennial plant that is usually grown as an annual, there are a number of cultivars of Chinese broccoli that vary in stem colour (from pale to medium green) and length.

Cultivation Chinese broccoli does best in a fertile soil that is rich in organic matter and is very well drained. It prefers soil with a pH 6 – 7 and daytime maximums of 18° – 28°C but will tolerate several degrees of frost so can be grown in most of Australia. It grows well in tropical regions, but as cool temperatures are necessary for flower development it is only grown as a winter crop. In more southern regions, very cool weather may cause Chinese broccoli to flower early. Grow from seed either sown directly into a prepared garden bed or into a seed tray. Sow the seed about half a centimetre deep. It will germinate in three to 10 days. If sown directly into the garden, then thin at about three weeks so that there is about 15 cm between plants. The thinnings can be used in salads or stir-fries. Spacing plants too far apart will cause the stems to become too thick and tough. In some parts of Asia, Chinese broccoli plants are sown very close together and then harvested while immature. Plants are shallow-rooted so make sure they are well watered in dry weather.

Chinese broccoli takes about nine weeks before the first florets are ready to harvest. Harvest the flower heads complete with stem and three to four young leaves just as the flowers begin to open. Use a sharp knife and leave other growth buds so that future cuts can be made. The best flavoured florets are those harvested well before the flower buds open, but the flavour is still good once a few flowers are open. Water with a weak solution of seaweed fertiliser after harvesting to encourage new growth, and the more regularly the florets are harvested the more will be produced.

Use The flower stalk, unopened flower buds and the tender leaves are all eaten, either whole or chopped. The long stems are generally split lengthwise to allow them to cook more rapidly. The fresh, slightly bitter flavour enhances soups, noodle and stir-fry dishes in China, while in Vietnam they are used in stir-fries, usually with beef, and steamed as a vegetable. The whole plant is high in calcium and iron, as well as having good levels of vitamins A and C, thiamine and potassium.

Brassica rapa Chinensis Group Brassicaceae
syn. *B. rapa* var. *chinensis*

Chinese white cabbage, white cabbage, Chinese celery cabbage, mustard cabbage, celery mustard

paak tsoi, pak toi, pak choi, bok choi, bok choy (ChC); peh-chai (ChH); bai cai, qing cai, xiao bai cai (ChM); sawi hijau (In); chingensai, shakushina, taisin (Ja); spey saa (Kh); phak kat khao (La); bok choy, sawi-puteh (Ma); pechay (Ph); phak kwang tung (Th); cai be trang (Vi)

These cabbages probably originated in eastern Asia and are now grown extensively in China, Japan, Malaysia and Indonesia. They are also grown commercially in all Australian states.

Description This non-heading form of Chinese cabbage has thick, white, crisp leaf stalks and veins and glossy, smooth, broad, dark green leaves that form a loose cluster and do not have serrated edges.

There are also cultivars, known collectively as green pak choi, with stems that are pale green instead of white, and leaves that are a paler green colour. There are a large number of cultivars of Chinese white cabbage. Cold season cultivars include 'Chinese White' and 'Soup Spoon'. Heat tolerant cultivars include 'Shanghai' and 'Canton'; a dwarf cultivar that is bolt resistant is 'Mei Quing', and one that has broader white stems is 'Joi Choi'.

Cultivation Chinese white cabbage is a cool season crop that does best in rich loamy soils with lots of organic matter. It can be grown as a winter crop in the tropics. It likes full sun, moist soils and is relatively frost-tolerant. Sow Chinese white cabbage in spring and autumn in cool regions, so they are growing when daytime maximums are 15° – 20°C. Some cultivars can be grown outside this temperature range because they are more heat- or cold-tolerant. Even so, long summer days and high temperatures may cause the leaves to become tough. This cabbage is shallow-rooted so it needs to be watered regularly during dry weather, and prefers a soil pH of 6.5 – 7. Transplanted seedlings will sometimes bolt to seed, so it is better to sow seed directly into the ground at a depth of 1 cm. Germination takes about seven days and optimum soil temperatures for germination are around 18°C. Thin plants to about 25 cm apart in each direction, and use the thinnings in salads and stir-fries. Plants are often harvested quite young, starting when they are only 15 cm tall with about eight leaves.

Use Young leaves and stems of Chinese white cabbage are eaten fresh in salads but they are also cooked in a wide range of dishes. Add chopped leaves and stems to soups and stir-fries a few minutes before serving. Braised, steamed or simmered, the whole plant (except for the root) is served as a vegetable, sometimes accompanied by a white sauce. The flavour is delicate, mild and refreshing with a slight hotness. The white stems are as important as the green leaves, but usu-

ally take longer to cook and have a milder, almost bland flavour. Slits or cuts in the stem hasten cooking. In China, the leaves and stems are pickled in salt for later use; they are also dried and added to soup in winter. Chinese white cabbage is high in vitamin C and dietary fibre and also provides some potassium.

Chinese white cabbage, Green pak choi

Brassica rapa Chinensis Group Brassicaceae
syn. *B. rapa* var. *parachinensis*

Chinese flowering cabbage, flowering white cabbage, false pak choy, mock pak choy

tsoi sum, paak tsoi sum, choi sum (ChC); chai-sim (ChH); cai xin, cai tai (ChM); sawi (Ma)

Grown commercially in all Australian states this cabbage comes originally from eastern Asia but is now cultivated in most countries around the world, particularly China, Japan, Malaysia and Indonesia.

Description Chinese flowering cabbage is a form of cabbage closely related to Chinese white cabbage (see page 38), but grown more for its flower stems than its leaves. There are several different cultivars and it is best to grow the one suited to the local climate. This is an annual plant with ovate-rounded fresh green, non-serrated leaves and rounded stems that grow at the base of the thick flower stem.

Plants in flower. The flower heads and leaves are usually harvested before the flowers are fully open.

Cultivation Chinese flowering cabbage does best in cool climates with relatively uniform conditions. It needs reasonable moisture and full sun. It will bolt to seed and flowering stems will be tough and less sweet if conditions get too hot. Most cultivars are not frost-tolerant, although a purple cultivar can withstand air temperatures down to -5°C. This cabbage does best in fertile, well-drained soils with a pH of 6 – 7. Water well and regularly during dry weather. Grow from seed sown either directly into the ground or into punnets with seedlings later transplanted. Seed germination takes between two and 10 days depending on the time of year but optimum soil temperatures are 21°C. Thin seedlings to 10 cm between plants and start harvesting plants after about 30 days, when the first flower buds begin to open. The whole flowering stem with leaves and flowers is harvested.

Use Use thinnings and young leaves in salads as well as young flower heads and open flowers. The whole plant (except for the root) is edible with a slightly bitter flavour. Roughly chop the stems and

40

flower heads and steam, boil or fry. Older stems may need to be peeled. Chinese flowering cabbage is particularly good in stir-fries and soups but be careful not to overcook it or the stems will loose their crispness. This cabbage is high in carotene, calcium and dietary fibre and also provides some potassium.

Brassica rapa Chinensis Group Brassicaceae syn. *B. rapa* var. *rosularis*

Chinese flat cabbage, flowering cabbage, flat black cabbage

taai koo tsoi, tai koo choi (ChC); wu ta cai, ta ge cai, tai gu cai, hei cai, piao er cai (ChM); tatsoi, tasai (Ja); spey khiev muul (Kh); phak kat som (La); choy sum (Ma); phak kwang tung do (Th); cai ngot bong (Vi)

This cabbage is probably of very early origin and it has been grown in China for many hundreds of years.

Description Chinese flat cabbage grows with glossy, very dark green, spoon-shaped leaves and white stems that lie flat on the ground. There are now numerous varieties and cultivars of this cabbage that vary in their uprightness, stem width and leaf colour.

Cultivation Sow seed directly where it is to grow from early spring to autumn. This variety of cabbage is resistant to frost and snow. In tropical regions it is a winter crop. Sow seed 1 cm deep in any good, nutrient-rich soil. Seed will germinate in about seven days with optimum soil temperatures of 21°C. Thin to about 20 cm between plants. These cabbages are cultivated in the same way as Chinese white cabbages (see page 38), the main difference is that they are less likely to bolt during hot weather.

Use Use in the same way as Chinese white cabbage (see page 38) except that the flavour is slightly stronger. Also the leaves grow right on the ground so must be washed carefully to get rid of any grit.

Brassica rapa Japonica Group Brassicaceae
syn. *B. rapa* var. *nipposinica*

mizuna, Japanese mustard, pot herb mustard, kyona

shui cai (ChM); mizuna, kyona, kyomizuna (Ja)

A traditional salad green in Japan, mizuna is grown commercially in New South Wales, Queensland and Victoria.

Description This annual or biennial salad plant grows in a dense clump to a height of 50 cm. The leaves are bright green and deeply indented with long white stems. If allowed to go to seed, the flowers are typically four-petalled and yellow. They are followed by typical 'mustard' seed, but these seeds do not have the pungency of some other mustards. Mibuna or mibu greens (also included in *Brassica rapa* Japonica Group) are very similar to mizuna except that the leaves have smooth edges.

Cultivation Mizuna and mibuna both grow easily from seed and if planted every couple of months will provide fresh leaves all year round. Plants are frost-tolerant and will grow in most soils, but the leaves are more tender in good soil. They do best in a nutrient-rich, well-drained soil with plenty of sun. Sow seed in spring and autumn and thin plants to a spacing of about 25 cm. Start harvesting the outside leaves as soon as they are big enough to use. Cut whole plants once they are about six weeks old but always leave some to go to seed so that new plants can be grown in the next season. In the tropics, these plants are grown as a winter crop; plant seed in autumn.

Mizuna

Mibuna

Use   The leaves of both mizuna and mibuna have a fresh, slightly mustardy flavour, and can be used from tiny seedlings to fully grown. The flavour of mibuna is a little stronger than that of mizuna. In Japan, the leaves from both plants are eaten in salads, soups, steamed dishes and stir-fries. In Australia, they are often sold in leafy vegetable and salad mixes. The flowering stems can also be eaten.

Brassica rapa   Pekinensis Group   Brassicaceae syn. *B. rapa* var. *pekinensis*

Chinese cabbage, celery cabbage, pe-tsai

shu tsoi, wong nga paak, bok choy, wong bok, siew choy (ChC); peh-chai (ChH); da bai cai, huang ya cai, jie qiu bai cai (ChM); sawi puteh, pecai (In); hakusai, nappa (Ja); spey kdaop (Kh); phak kat khao (La); sawi puteh (Ma); phak kat khao (Th); cai lam kim chi (Vi)

This cabbage has been grown in Asia at least since the 5th century and probably comes originally from eastern Asia. It is grown commercially in all Australian states.

Description   Generally this cabbage grows with white fleshy stems and broad, flat, light greenish-yellow, crinkled leaves. The leaves are erect and overlap to form a compact head. Over 200 different varieties are grown in China, with different varieties for different regions from temperate to tropical.   Most commonly, Chinese cabbage falls into three different types — tall cylindrical types, barrel types and flowery hearted types. Tall cylindrical types form a dense head of pale green leaves with a white mid-rib on the outside and creamy yellow leaves towards the centre. Unlike ordinary cabbages, these heads are longer than they are wide, often 40 cm long and 10 – 15 cm wide. Some cultivars of this type are 'Chihili', 'Michihli', 'Market Pride', 'Shantung', 'Shaho Tsai'. Barrel types form compact more rounded heads made up of leaves with white mid-ribs and slightly greener leaves. Some cultivars of this type are 'Che-foo', 'Wong Bok', 'Spring Giant', 'Tokyo Giant', 'Tropical Pride', 'Early Top', 'Tip Top', 'China King', 'Winter Giant', 'Oriental King' and 'Winter Knight'. Flowery hearted types have leaves that form a loose but dense cluster that range in colour from white in the centre to green on the outside. Quite often the outer leaves are curved outwards.

Cultivation   Chinese cabbages need a deep, well-drained soil but they are not fussy as to whether it is sandy or heavy

43

loam. They do best in nutrient-rich soils with a pH of 5.5 – 7, and full sun. Optimal daytime maximum temperatures for good head production are about 16°C. Much lower temperatures will cause plants to bolt to seed, while much higher temperatures will produce narrow leaves which may be soft and bitter.

The best time to sow Chinese cabbage in temperate regions is late summer and autumn. Early spring is also suitable in frost-free areas. In tropical regions, seed can only be sown in autumn for winter growth. Seed germinates in about three days at soil temperatures close to 20°C. It can be sown directly into the garden, or into punnets and transplanted when seedlings are about three weeks old. Transplanted seedlings will sometimes bolt to seed. Space plants about 35 cm apart. Keep weed free. Add animal manure to the soil a few weeks before planting, and top dress with more manure at about five weeks. Plants need regular water.

Commercially, this cabbage is harvested when the heads are firm and well filled but not too hard. This can take up to 100 days. Barrel types mature more quickly than tall cylindrical types. In the home garden Chinese cabbage can be harvested at any stage, and young plants are useful 'cut and come again' vegetables. To do this, cut the leaves leaving the very small central leaves. The plant will continue to grow from these.

'Wong bok' hybrid

Use This cabbage has a sweet flavour and crisp texture quite different to European cabbages. Leaves are chopped and used in salads, stir-fries and soups, or just cooked as a vegetable. Never overcook or the flavour will be destroyed. The leaves are also used to wrap other ingredients. Chinese cabbage is a major source of vitamins for the Chinese people, especially during winter, because the cabbages store well in cold weather. In Korea, Chinese cabbage is fermented to make *kimchi*, a popular side dish. This is made by layering Chinese cabbage, radish, garlic, hot pepper and salt in large earthenware jars. This cabbage is also an important ingredient of several Japanese dishes including sukiyaki.

Barrel type

Brassica rapa Perviridis Group Brassicaceae
syn. *B. rapa* var. *perviridis*

komatsuna, spinach mustard, tendergreen, Japanese mustard

komatsuna (Ja)

This brassica has been widely grown in Japan for many hundreds of years, but it is virtually unknown in China. Today there are a range of different komatsuna cultivars gown in Japan. Some of these have been obtained by crossing with other closely related brassicas like Chinese cabbage, Chinese white cabbage and Japanese turnip.

Description   Komatsuna is a hardy, upright plant that grows over 1 m tall. It has oval, oblong leaves that are dark green and about 25 cm long and 15 cm wide. Flowers are yellow and typically four-petalled.

Cultivation   Grow from seed sown in a sunny position any time from spring to late autumn. Komatsuna is a cool climate plant that grows well in temperate and subtropical regions. It can be grown in the winter in some tropical regions. Seed should germinate in about seven days at soil temperatures of 12°C. Add animal manure to the soil a few weeks before planting, and top-dress with more manure at about five weeks. Space plants about 30 cm apart. Keep weed free and water regularly. Young plants are ready to harvest about six weeks after sowing when they are about 20 cm high. These brassicas are very cold-tolerant.

Use   Komatsuna is rich in vitamins, and tastes like a combination of Chinese cabbage and spinach with a hint of mustard. Eat young leaves in salads and add to soups or stir-fries, or simply cook as a vegetable in the same way that Chinese cabbage is cooked. The Japanese also pickle the leaves.

Brassica rapa Rapifera Group Brassicaceae
syn. *B. rapa* var. *rapifera*

Japanese turnip

mo ching (ChC); wujing, manjing (ChM); kabu, kabura (Ja)

Turnips also belong in the brassica family, even though it is the turnip root that is usually eaten, rather than the leaf. Japanese turnip is superficially similar to European turnips but has ancestors and a long history of cultivation that are quite separate. This has resulted in the cells of Japanese turnips having less chromosomes than those of European turnips.

Description Japanese turnips grow from swollen roots with short, branching stems and ragged-edged, rounded leaves. Traditionally, there are two different forms of Japanese turnip — small or kok-abu turnips and large or okabu turnips. There are several different cultivars of each that vary in both colour and shape. Probably the most commonly seen are the small, rounded kokabu types.

Cultivation Japanese turnips grow in most soils and do best in regions with mild temperatures. Grow from seed sown in early spring, late summer and autumn where the plants are to grow and in a sunny position. Thin to about 20 cm between plants. Keep plants well watered to encourage constant, quick growth. Kokabu types are harvested about 40 days after sowing, while obaku types take 60 – 100 days depending on the size desired. Harvest, and use the whole plant as soon as possible because they rapidly lose their crispness once harvested.

Use Both the roots and leaves are eaten, with the leaves being rich in carotene and calcium. In Japan, the roots are eaten fresh in salads, or cooked in the same way as daikon radishes (see page 117), or they are pickled. Young leaves can be cooked as a vegetable by frying, steaming or braising. They can also be added to salads, soups and stir-fries.

Mini turnip, 'Tokyo Cross', kokabu type
(photograph courtesy Digger's Seeds)

Cajanus cajan   Fabaceae

pigeon pea, congo bean

pesinngon (Bu); katjang goode (In); kachang kayu (Ma); tua re (Th)

A native of India and a commercially important crop there, pigeon peas are also widely cultivated in other tropical countries. They have been in use in South-East Asia for more than 500 years.

Description   This woody, perennial, leguminous shrub grows to about 2 m high with wiry, slender branches and narrow leaves that occur in threes. Yellow flowers are followed by dark grey or yellow seeds growing in bright green pods. There are different cultivars varying in height including some new dwarf cultivars, but all are heavy bearers.

Cultivation   In tropical regions, seed is sown at the beginning of the wet season and peas can be harvested about four months later. Harvesting can continue for most of the year, but bushes will need to be pruned at least once a year and top-dressed with manure at the same time, to ensure a good crop the following year. In temperate regions, this plant is grown as an annual because it is killed by frost. Sow seed in late spring and early summer once the soil has warmed up. Wherever it is being grown, plant seeds about 2 cm deep in groups of two or three in raised beds. Plants need to be about 1 m apart. This plant grows easily in hot regions, is very drought resistant and has the added benefit of adding nutrients to the soil. Like

Pigeon pea showing the leaves, flowers and young developing pods

other legumes, the plant roots host bacteria that absorb nitrogen from the air and convert it to soluble nitrates. Recent research shows that the roots of pigeon peas give off a chemical that dissolves iron phosphates in the soil, making the phosphate available to be taken up by plant roots. In India, pigeon peas are often intercropped with other crops.

Use Both young green pods with immature seeds and fully mature seeds are eaten. The young green pods can be treated in the same way as common peas. Mature pigeon peas are usually dried and used as a pulse; their sweet flavour makes them ideal for curries and vegetable soups. In India they are known as toor dhal. Peas can also be sprouted. Pigeon peas contain more minerals, five times more vitamin A and three times more vitamin C than ordinary peas. Their protein content can be as high as 28%, making them an excellent food for vegetarians. In parts of Asia, the wood from the bushes is used as firewood, and branches are used for thatching and basketmaking. The leaves are also fed to stock and are a source of food for silkworms.

Canna indica Cannaceae

edible canna, achira, Australian arrowroot, Queensland arrowroot, gruya, purple arrowroot

adalut (Bu); ganyong, lembong njeedra, seneetra (In); ganyong, kenyong, ubi gereda (Ma); zembu (Ph); sakhu chin (Th); cu chuoi, dong rieng (Vi)

Edible canna comes originally from the Andes of South America. Cooked tubers have been found in tombs in this region from as long ago as 2500 BC. Although it is not often used in South America today, except as an emergency food source, it has gained great acceptance in some Asian countries, especially Vietnam. In North Vietnam, large areas of canna are grown for the purpose of extracting starch from the tubers. The starch is then used to make high grade transparent starch noo-

dles. In the 1940s this crop was grown commercially in Queensland.

Description This tropical plant grows to more than 3 m with oblong green leaves that can be 60 cm long and 30 cm wide. Flowers are bright red to orange and very decorative. Its roots are thick rhizomes which grow large, rounded, edible tubers. *C. indica* 'Purpurea' has dark green and purple leaves and red flowers.

Cultivation Edible canna is very easy to grow in the tropics and mild temperate regions. It likes full sun but will tolerate some shade. Propagate by separating underground rhizomes and planting out with at least two growth buds. Completely bury the rhizome and leave at least 60 cm between plants. Edible canna will grow in low nutrient soils and doesn't need much water, although roots are larger and more tender if the plant is regularly watered. It can be grown in regions that are degraded by erosion to help reduce damage. First harvest is possible about six months after planting, but maximum yield is obtained if the harvest is left to eight to ten months,

when some of the plants will be in flower. Any rhizomes not needed can be left in the ground and harvested all year round. In cooler regions, the plant dies back in winter.

Use Rhizomes are dug, washed and eaten raw, or they can be boiled, baked and added to soup. The Vietnamese call this root 'cu choi' which means 'banana root'. The roots are also used to produce starch. To do this they are shredded or grated and dropped into water. The fibrous pulp is separated from the heavier starch by decanting. The starch is then used in foods; it is clear rather than opaque when cooked and is easily digestible. Young shoots are also eaten and the leaves used to wrap food when baking. The whole plant also makes a useful stock food, especially for pigs, and can be grown as an effective screen or windbreak in frost-free areas. Canna rhizomes contain starch and sugar, as well as protein and potassium and smaller amounts of calcium and phosphorous.

Capsicum spp. Solanaceae

C. annuum Cerasiforme Group: bird's-eye pepper, cherry pepper; Longum Group: cayenne pepper, chilli pepper
C. frutescens chilli pepper, tabasco pepper

lup chew (ChC); la jiao (ChM); cabai, lombok (In); mteh (Kh); mak phet (La); cili, cabai, chabai, lada merah (Ma); phrik (Th); ot (Vi)

Chilli peppers are an essential part of most Asian cooking, but they are not native to Asia. They were introduced to tropical Asia by the Portuguese in the 1500s, but come originally from Central and South America, where they are still widely cultivated. Prehistoric remains of this plant have been found in Peru.

Description Most chilli peppers grow on branched perennial shrubs that can be 1 – 2 m in height. The stems are woody at the base, while the leaves are glossy, dark green and an elongated heart shape. Small greenish-white flowers occur singly or in groups of two or three throughout the season. These are followed by small, green, orange, yellow or red fruit. The fruits contain numerous seeds, usually at the basal end. Ten or more different chillies are commonly used in Asian countries. They range from tiny bird's eye chillies known in Thailand as 'rat droppings', through plump rounded chillies of various colours to finger length chillies which can be picked when they are green or red.

The chemical capsaicin, found in chillies, is the reason for the very hot taste of the flesh and seeds.

Cultivation Grow chilli pepper bushes from seed sown in spring into punnets. Seeds sprout most rapidly at soil temperatures of about 21°C. Transplant once the seedlings are big enough to move — generally about eight weeks later. Chilli peppers like the same conditions as tomatoes — full sun, and a well-drained soil with added animal manure. Plants are cold and frost-tender, so in cold regions they are all grown as annuals. A late cold snap will set plants back and they will often be slow to recover. In the tropics, they can be grown all year round, and *C. frutescens* cultivars will grow for many years and develop into substantial bushes. Prune these types once a year (generally in winter) and feed regularly. Chilli peppers can be harvested at any stage of development, but as a rule the longer they are left and the redder they are the hotter they are. Once fully mature they are sweeter, will keep better and can be dried with less chance of rotting.

To dry chillies, leave them on the bush until they are fully matured and even slightly shrivelled, then pick and dry in the sun on a hot, dry day, or days. Once dry, store in a tightly sealed jar out of direct light. In cooler regions, where cold, wet weather may cause the chillies to rot before they have fully matured, dig up the whole plant and hang it in a sheltered airy position. The chillies will continue to ripen for up to a month. Dry in the sun if possible, but if not then use a warm oven.

Use Hot chilli peppers are widely used in Asian cooking. Red and green chillies have different flavours and fragrances so they are not interchangeable in recipes. Chillies are added to sauces, soups and stews as well as curries. Fresh chillies are made into dipping sauces by grinding them with other ingredients like garlic and ginger, then adding vinegar, water and sugar and simmering for a few minutes and leaving to cool. Finely sliced, they are used as a garnish. Dried chillies are used in cooking by cutting into about 2 cm lengths and soaking in warm water until soft, then pounding to a paste before cooking. Most of the heat is in the seeds, so the amount of heat in the dish can be controlled by removing some or all of the seeds. Dried chillies can also be pickled or steeped in oil, and the oil is then used, especially in Chinese cooking, to prepare a range of dishes. In Thailand they are dry-fried until crisp and then ground into a powder to be used as a condiment. Dried and powdered, chillies are added to curry powder. Always handle chillies with care. Try not to handle cut surfaces, and when finished always wash your hands in cold water. Never touch your eyes after handling chillies and don't touch children either. Fresh chillies are rich in vitamins A and C.

Bird's eye chilli

Centella asiatica   Hydrocotylaceae

gotu cola, Indian pennywort, Asian pennywort

di qien cao (ChM); pegagan (In); rom chang (Kh); phak nok (La); daun pegaga (Ma); bua bok (Th); rau ma (Vi)

Gotu cola has a long medicinal history, and is believed in many Asian countries to improve memory and prolong life. A Chinese professor was reputed long ago to have lived to 265 as the result of drinking tea made from gotu cola leaves.

Description   This creeping perennial plant grows to only 20 cm. It puts out slender stolons with distinct nodes. Roots and clumps of round, heart-shaped, crinkled leaves grow from these nodes as the plant spreads over the ground. The flowers are red or purple-red in colour; these are followed by flattened fruit.

Cultivation   Grow gotu cola from seed sown in spring, or by division in spring or autumn. Place plants about 30 cm apart. This herb does best in moist ground but will also tolerate dry periods. It is not fussy about soil and will do well in sun or semi-shade. In cooler regions, gotu cola becomes dormant in winter with little or no growth, and it may even die back. In spring it will start to grow rapidly again, and under ideal conditions may become a pest. In warmer tropical regions grow gotu cola in a shady position and keep well watered in winter.

Use   Gotu cola is commonly used as a vegetable and a medicine. In Vietnam, leaves are added fresh to soups, eaten raw as part of a salad and ground and mixed with sugar to make a very sweet drink. The leaves can also be steamed and added to rice or used as a garnish on soups and stews. Medicinally, gotu cola is regarded as being useful in improving blood circulation, in reducing inflammation in arthritis, stimulating hair and nail growth, helping to cure skin diseases and in making people live longer. This herb should not be eaten regularly by anyone with high blood pressure or anyone who is taking blood-thinning drugs.

Chrysanthemum coronarium var. *spatiosum*   Asteraceae

garland chrysanthemum, edible chrysanthemum, vegetable chrysanthemum, chop suey greens, Japanese greens

tung ho, tong ho choi, chong ho, tong-mo (ChC); tang-oh (ChH); tung hao, hao zi gan (ChM); shungiku, shingiku, kikuna (Ja); sukkat (Ko); tong ho, kek wah (Ma); tan o, cai cuc (Vi)

Garland chrysanthemum comes originally from the Mediterranean, parts of Europe and northern Asia, but is now widely grown and naturalised in the cooler highland tropical regions of South-East Asia, China and Japan.

Description This chrysanthemum is an annual that grows initially from a single, tender, round stalk with finely-cut, green leaves. If not harvested, the plants will grow to 1 m and develop daisy-like yellow flowers over a long period. The flowers of the most common form are golden yellow in the centre and pale creamy-yellow on the outside. There are several cultivars that vary in leaf shape and size.

Cultivation Garland chrysanthemums grow well in temperate regions and in highland regions in the tropics. In tropical climates they can be grown in winter. Grow from seed sown in shallow trenches in early spring or autumn. They take about seven days to germinate. Thin plants to about 15 cm apart. Garland chrysanthemum grows best in a nutrient and humus-rich soil in full sun. Plants need to be watered regularly. Pick the first leaves about 30 days after sowing. Leaves

are at their best when plants are young, as they become bitter as the plant ages, or in very hot weather. Remove the flower heads from most of the plants to encourage more leaf growth, but allow a couple to flower so the flowers can be picked and used. Garland chrysanthemums grow well in pots and can be regularly resown.

Use Eat the strongly aromatic leaves and stems as a vegetable. Steam, blanch or boil in a tiny amount of water and serve with a little soy sauce and sesame oil. Don't overcook as this makes them bitter. In Japan, garland chrysanthemum leaves are an important ingredient in one pot beef and fish dishes. If they are to be used on their own they are usually dipped briefly into boiling water and then plunged into cold water to maintain the green colour. In Korea, the leaves are used with strongly flavoured fish to neutralise the flavour and in China, they are added to soups and stir-fries. The Vietnamese use the leaves in chicken, pork and beef dishes and fried as a vegetable. Fresh young leaves are high in vitamin A and are an interesting ingredient in leafy salads. Sprouted seeds are also eaten in salads or as a snack. In Japan, the petals are used either fresh or dried in salads, with fish, and in soups and pickles.

Citrus hystrix Rutaceae

kaffir lime, leech lime, caffre lime, wild lime

shauk-nu, shauk-waing (Bu); daun jeruk purut (In); krauch soeuch (Kh); daun limau purut (Ma); bai magrut, bai makrut (Th); la chanh (Vi)

Kaffir lime belongs to the same group of trees as the lemon. This citrus group has been cultivated for so long that it is not now possible to be certain of their country of origin, but they probably originate from somewhere in Asia. Kaffir limes are traditionally thought to ward off evil spirits.

Description Kaffir lime grows as a small tree to about 4 m with distinctive double, glossy green leaves. The fruit are dark green, warty and contain almost no juice. Fully developed they are about 9 cm long and 5 cm wide. The leaves and fruit both have a distinct, sharp, lemon taste and smell.

Cultivation In tropical regions, kaffir limes can be grown outside in well-drained nutrient-rich soil in full sun. Dig in some well-rotted manure and blood and bone before planting, and mulch with compost and straw after planting, but be careful not to mulch too close to the trunk. Keep well watered during dry periods, and foliar feed by spraying seaweed fertiliser on the leaves several times during spring and summer. Like other citrus it will benefit from an addition of iron chelates once a year. In cooler regions, plant kaffir lime in a large pot in a warm sunny position and move to a more sheltered, north-facing position in winter. Leaves can be harvested all year round, and fruit when it ripens as there is no specific time for fruit production.

Use Both the grated rind or 'zest' of the fruit, and the leaves, are added to a range of Asian dishes. They have a marvellous, aromatic, citrusy scent and flavour that is unique and cannot really be replaced by other citrus plants. The leaves can be shredded or used whole and then removed. Usually the softer leaf blade is pulled away from the hard central stem before use. Add a leaf to a dish at the beginning of cooking and it will gradually release its flavour during the cooking process. In Thailand, some dishes (for example tom yam soup) cannot be made without kaffir lime leaf. Shredded, fresh leaves are added to salads and cooked vegetable dishes, as well as dishes like beef stir-fry and fish curries. In Malaysia and Singapore, they are used in combination with other fresh herbs. Indonesians use these lime leaves to flavour soy sauce. Leaves do not dry well but they can be kept in the freezer for long periods. Small pieces of rind add a sharp, sour flavour to curry pastes that are used in a range of Thai dishes. Dry the zest by cutting it off

(photograph by H.F. Chin)

the fruit and spreading it out on a plate until completely dry. Store in a well-sealed jar, to be reconstituted when needed by soaking in water. Whole limes can also be frozen. The juice from the fruit is used in soaps and shampoos.

Colocasia esculenta   Araceae

taro, dasheen, elephant's ear, edo, cocoyam

Tuber: wu tau, oo tau, woo, wu chai (ChC); yu, yu tou, yu nai (ChM); talas (In); sato-imo, kiomo (Ja); keladi (Ma); gabi (Ph); puak (Th); khoai mon (Vi)
Stem: tales (In); bon, kok thoune (La); keladi (Ma); phuak (Th); bac ha (Vi)

Taro is a food staple for the people of the South Pacific and is widely grown in tropical regions throughout the world including Asia. This is a very ancient crop plant that may have been cultivated for more than 9000 years. Taro was often carried by travellers because it keeps really well after drying. Commercial crops are grown in New South Wales, Queensland and Northern Territory.

Description   A perennial plant, taro grows from tuberous roots that produce small side growths known as cormels. It grows with erect purple or green stems that can be up to 1 m long. The leaves can be very large (hence the name elephant's ear), ovate and are purple or green. Plants do not often flower, but if they do the flower is usually green and yellow and is followed by green berries.

Cultivation   Taro does well in most soils as long as they are nutrient-rich and the pH is 5.5 – 7. It is a heavy feeder so add manure before planting. Since taro rarely flowers it is usually grown by planting tubers with some growth points. These growth points are small knobs on the skin of the tuber.

Plant the tubers so they are covered by about 6 cm of soil about 35 cm apart.

Water liberally — don't worry about some waterlogging — and add more manure when plants are about 60 cm high. If taro is being grown in water then it should be no more than 15 cm deep and regularly topped up with fresh water. Taro is a tropical or subtropical plant that must have a long hot summer (optimum daytime maximums of 25 – 35°C) and at least 200 days to develop large tubers. It does not tolerate heavy frosts, while light frosts will cause it to die back, but it will usually reshoot in spring. Harvest the tubers when the leaves start to yellow in autumn. The entire tuber should be very firm. They can remain in the soil until needed as long as there is no chance of heavy frost. If all the tubers are harvested then save the small cormels and plant these, in the same way as tubers, for next year's crop. Don't let these cormels dry out. It is not possible to grow taro for its tubers in cool climates because it is just not hot enough for long enough. Taro, however, is an attractive plant in its own right and cultivars with edible stems can be grown in cooler regions. Harvest taro stems at any time, but they are at their best in spring and summer.

Use   Taro should never be eaten raw, as all parts contain calcium oxalate which is made up of sharp crystals that cause intense irritation to the inside of the mouth and tongue. This dissipates with cooking. Modern cultivars have very low calcium oxalate content, and most of this is found in the skin, so always peel tubers first. Leaves and stems are eaten and there are some cultivars of taro that are grown specifically for their stems rather than the tubers. Eat only young leaves and always boil leaves and stems before eating. They are high in calcium, potassium and vitamin A. Cooked leaves are sometimes used to wrap other ingredients and then steamed. Stems are usually peeled, cut into short sections and boiled. In Vietnam, they are added to sour fish soups. Most taro cultivars are grown for their tubers; these can be roasted, fried, baked, braised, mashed, sauteed or boiled. Always dry peel the tubers and wipe clean. Do not soak in water or they will become slimy. The flavour is similar to sweet potatoes, but the texture is drier. Chips made from taro roots have a delicious nutty flavour. The Chinese use taro in a range of dishes including desserts. Grains of starch in taro tubers are the smallest in any plant and this makes them very easily digestible. Taro tubers are higher in proteins than potatoes but are used mainly for their starch content. They are also rich in vitamins B and C as well as calcium, iron and phosphorous.

Taro tubers

Taro grown for stems

Coriandrum sativum Apiaceae

coriander, cilantro, Chinese parsley

nan nan bin (Bu); yuen sai (ChC); wan sui (ChH); yuen sai, yuan cai (ChM); ketumbar (In); koyen-doro (Ja); van suy (Kh); phak hom pom (La); ketumbar (Ma); wansuey (Ph); phak chi, pak chee (Th); ngo (Vi)

Coriander is one of the most ancient herbs still in use today, and claimed by some to be the world's most widely used herb. Whether this is true or not, coriander leaves and seeds are essential to the cuisine of central and southern America, South-East and northern Asia as well as India and the Middle East. Coriander comes originally from southern Europe where the seeds have been used for a long time, but the leaves were not usually used. Coriander seeds have been found in Egyptian tombs dating from more than 3000 years ago. The botanical and common name, coriander, comes from the Greek word *koris* which means 'bug'. This presumably relates to the fact that the smell and flavour of coriander has been unfavourably compared with that of stink bugs.

Description This erect annual herb has lower leaves that are rounded and lobed, while the upper leaves are linear and finely dissected. Small flat umbels of pale pink flowers appear from midsummer, and these are followed by fruits that are small green berries and which become brown and ridged when fully ripe. The whole plant contains a fragrant volatile oil. There are now several cultivars that vary in flavour, size and tendency to bolt to seed in hot conditions.

Cultivation Grow coriander from seed sown in spring or autumn. Plant the seed where it is to grow because it does not transplant well. Thin to about 15 cm between plants. In areas with hot, dry summers, seedlings will go to seed very quickly, so in these places coriander is best planted in autumn. Coriander does well in any good, nutrient-rich soil that is well drained. In very hot regions it can be grown in the shade, but in cooler regions grow it in full sun. Keep well watered. Start harvesting leaves after about 30

days. Leaves have the best flavour while the stems are still soft and before the flowers start to form. Whole plants can be harvested for their roots at the same time. Seeds are harvested as they start to turn from green to brown. Cut off the whole seed head and hang upside down in a paper bag, in a dry, airy, shaded position. When the seeds are dry, strip them from the stems and store in an airtight container out of direct light.

Use Coriander is a nutritious herb rich in calcium, phosphorous, beta carotene and vitamin C. It has an unusual, very strong taste when fresh, and both the leaves and roots are commonly used in Asian cooking. Leaves are used as garnish and to add fragrance to soups, meat dishes and particularly fish dishes. They are always added towards the end of the cooking process. The Chinese use leaves in dim sum stuffing and in soup. The Vietnamese use fresh coriander leaves in soups, salads and noodle dishes. Dried leaves do not retain their flavour. Thais add fresh roots to a range of dishes and a combination of coriander root, garlic and pepper all crushed together is an essential seasoning in many Thai dishes. The dried seed has a sweet, almost orangy, taste and is an important ingredient of most curry spice mixes. The flavour of the seeds is enhanced if they are lightly cooked in a dry frying pan and then crushed just before they are to be used.

Cryptotaenia canadensis Apiaceae

mitsuba, Japanese honewort, Japanese wild chervil, Japanese parsley, trefoil

san ip, sam ip (ChC); san ye qin, ya er qin (ChM); mitsuba (Ja)

Mitsuba is native to many countries in Asia, parts of Africa and eastern North America, but it is in Japan that it is regularly cultivated and used in a range of dishes.

Description This perennial leafy herb grows from a taproot to 70 cm with deeply divided, aromatic three-lobed leaves and tiny white flowers that occur in umbels at the top the plant.

shady position in tropical regions, but in cooler climates grows in full sun. Keep well watered during dry weather.

Cultivation Grow from seed sown in spring or autumn, but in frost-free regions seed can be sown all year round. Plant into a shallow trench in nutrient-rich moist soil and thin seedlings to about 15 cm apart. Begin to harvest once the stems are about 15 cm long and continue to harvest leaves for most of the year. Remove flower heads in autumn and trim the whole plant in spring and autumn to encourage more leafy growth. This herb grows best in a

Use Leaves, leaf stalks and roots are all used in a range of Japanese dishes including *sushi*, *tempura* and *sukiyaki*. The leaves are also added to egg dishes and foods pickled in vinegar. The Japanese frequently use this herb as a garnish, where one method is to knot three stems together and fan out the leaves, another is to mince the leaves and sprinkle over soups and cold noodle dishes. Leaves have a flavour somewhere between parsley and angelica, and can be used as a substitute for parsley in many dishes. Try sprinkling over rice and adding to green salads. The stems have slightly more flavour and are usually blanched and finely chopped before use. Sprouted seeds and very young seedlings are also eaten. Roots are carefully washed, blanched, coarsely chopped and then sauteed in sesame oil and soy sauce.

Cucurbita moschata and *Cucurbita maxima* Cucurbitaceae

Japanese pumpkin, winter squash, kabocha squash

nam kwa, fan kwa (ChC); nan gua (ChM); kabocha (Ja); labu merah (Ma); kalabasa (Ph); bi (Vi)

Japanese pumpkins are a type of pumpkin similar to those already widely grown in Western countries. These pumpkins have been mainly cultivated and developed in Japan but are now grown in many other Asian countries, including China, where they are seen as a fertility symbol. They are grown commercially in New South Wales, Queensland, Tasmania and Victoria.

Description Pumpkins grow as vigorous, long trailing plants with large, slightly lobed leaves, angular stems and branched tendrils. The flowers are yellow with male and female flowers occurring separately on the same plant. Japanese pumpkins are smooth skinned and usually dark green with paler green markings. The flesh is dry and sweet with a nutty flavour and is yellow or orange in colour. These pumpkins keep well. There are several cultivars grown commercially and available in Australia. These include 'Delica' (also known as Ebisu) and 'Kurijiman F1' that do well in Victoria, 'Pacifica' that does well in Queensland as well as 'Puccini', 'Late Potkin' and 'Tetsukabuto F1'.

Cultivation Sow seeds where they are to grow, about 3 cm below the surface, from spring to early summer in temperate regions, and early autumn to late winter in the tropics. Seeds take five to seven days to germinate and do so most readily at soil temperatures of 18° – 25°C. Space plants about 50 cm apart and 1.5 m from other plants. Pumpkins are heavy feeders so add lots of manure and compost before planting. They do best in soils with a pH of 6 – 7 although slightly more alkaline soils will be tolerated. Japanese pumpkins, like other pumpkins, need a long, hot growing season of at least three months. They do best in warm conditions, with daytime maximums of 20 – 30°C and night-time minimums of 15 – 20°C. Japanese pumpkins are more tolerant of high temperatures and tropical conditions than many other pumpkins and this is why they are the pumpkin most commonly grown in many Asian countries. They will not toler-ate frosts. Harvest pumpkins when they are fully mature — when the vine begins to die back in autumn.

Use Pumpkins are cooked as a vegetable by baking, steaming or boiling. They are also stir-fried with other vegetables or added to soups. They are always peeled first. The Japanese deep-fry pumpkin in *tempura* batter. A sweet Malaysian dish known as *pengat* is made using pumpkin with sweet potato or banana cooked in coconut milk.

Curcuma longa Zingiberaceae

turmeric

Sa-nwin (Bu); wong-keong (ChC); ng kiew (ChH); huang jiang (ChM); kunyit (In); ukon (Ja); romiet (Kh); khamin khune (La); kunyit (Ma); dilaw (Ph); kha-min (Th); nghe (Vi)

Turmeric comes originally from southern Asia but is now widely cultivated throughout the tropics. The recorded use of turmeric dates back to 600 BC in Assyria. In Europe, in the Middle Ages, it was known as Indian Saffron and the tuber was used to dye fabric. In Thailand, it signifies purity and sanctity and it is used to anoint novice monks.

Description Turmeric is a perennial that grows from a large rhizome surrounded by stalkless, cylindrical tubers that are bright yellow-orange inside. From the rhizome grow large, broad, oblong leaves and pseudo-stems up to 1 m. The occasional flowers occur in dense spikes which grow from the centre of the clumps and are pale yellow or white.

Cultivation Grow new plants from pieces of root with one or two buds. Plant in autumn or spring about 5 cm deep. Turmeric is a tropical plant that can be grown inside or in a greenhouse in more temperate regions. The rhizome will grow more quickly if the planting area is covered in clear plastic to maintain warmth and humidity — this is removed once shoots appear. Frequent misting with water will aid growth, and plants need a warm sunny position and regular addi-

tions of water. In tropical regions, turmeric is usually grown in areas with more than 1000 mm of rainfall a year. It likes a fertile, open, loamy soil that is well drained because it does not like to be waterlogged. The rhizomes are harvested in autumn.

Use In South-East Asia the rhizomes are usually used fresh. Fresh rhizomes are very strong in flavour so only a small amount is needed — often no bigger than a cubic centimetre. They are also often crushed first, to extract the orange-yellow juice that is then used. In Malaysia, rice coloured by cooking with turmeric, known as *nasi kunyit*, is eaten on ceremonial occasions. In Burma, a little turmeric is frequently added to vegetables. Fresh leaves are also added to some dishes, while young leaves, shoots and flowers can be boiled as a vegetable. Leaves are also used for wrapping other ingredients, especially fish, before steaming or roasting. Roots are also occasionally used dried and powdered. To dry first wash off any dirt, place in water, bring to the boil and simmer gently for about four hours or until the roots are tender. Remove and leave to dry in a sunny position until the roots are hard and brittle. Now grind the root to a powder. Powdered turmeric is

aromatic with a musky flavour; however, it is mainly used in cooking for its strong colour. It is added to mustards, curries, pickles, sauces and confectionery, and is an important ingredient of most curry spice mixes. It is also used as a dye for fabrics and in cosmetics.

Turmeric is used medicinally for its antiseptic and astringent properties. In India it is known as *haldi* and has been used by generations of Indians as the 'cure all' for cuts, scrapes and bruises.

Cymbopogon citratus   Poaceae

lemon grass

zabalin (Bu); heung maau tso (ChC); cang mao (ChH); xiang mao cao (ChM); serai, sereh (In); remon gurasu (Ja); sloeuk krey, bai mak nao (Kh); houa si khai (La); serai (Ma); tanglad (Ph); ta krai (Th); xa, sa (Vi)

Lemon-scented grasses are tropical plants found in northern Australia and South-East Asia. *C. citratus* probably comes originally from Malaysia.

Description The lemony leaves of lemon grass are typically grass-like, growing up to 1 m from bulbous stolons with translucent, arching leaf blades. Clumps often grow to 1 m across (see front cover). The plant rarely flowers. The whole plant has a delicious, sharp, lemon taste and flavour.

Cultivation Lemon grass grows easily in most tropical regions, needing little attention. It likes a nutrient-rich, well-drained soil and full sun. Propagate new plants by dividing clumps into groups of two or three stolons so that some roots are attached to each piece. Space new plants at least 50 cm apart. In tropical regions, new plants can be grown by placing a stem into water until roots begin to grow and then planting. Lemon grass can also be grown successfully in temperate regions as long as plants have a sheltered, warm, sunny position, with plenty of water in summer. A bad frost will severely retard or kill even a well-established plant, and wet, cold winters will make it look brown and straggly. Mulch well during hot summers and feed with well-rot-ted manure in early spring. Lemon grass grows well in a large pot.

Use The distinctive lemon fragrance of lemon grass leaf stems is essential to many Asian dishes. Harvest outside stems that are at least 1 cm across. If using it whole, just cut off the top leafy portion, bruise the base and add to the dish. Remove before serving. To slice or mince, use the bottom 15 cm or so of the stems, peeling away the outer layers until a pinkish colour appears. The tender centre is then finely sliced or minced. Alternatively the centre portion can be cooked and eaten with rice as a vegetable. Lemon grass is used to flavour curries and other dishes, and is particularly good in chicken soups. Minced, it can be added to stuffings for fish and chicken, or added to a marinade. In Vietnam, it is paired with garlic and used in a range of different stir-fries, while in Indonesia and Malaysia, it is often combined with fresh turmeric and shrimp paste. Wrap stems in plastic and freeze to store for later use. Dried lemon grass stems are not a good substitute for the fresh stems. Fresh or dried leaves are made into a delicious lemon-flavoured tea, and tied in a bunch they can be added to soups or stews to impart a subtle lemon flavour. Oil is extracted from the whole plant and used in perfumery. Where growth is prolific in tropical regions, lemon grass, citronella grass and other scented grasses are cut in autumn and used as a mulch during the dry season. This mulch helps to retain water, add nutrients and stop erosion during the wet season.

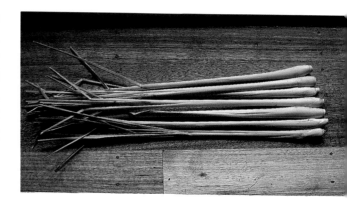

Dioscorea alata   Dioscoreaceae

yam, greater yam, greater Asiatic yam, white yam

dai shue, taai shue, tai shue (ChC); shu yu, shan yao (ChM); arvi, banda (In); yamaimo, nagaimo (Ja); keladi (Ma); ube, ubi (Ph)

This group of plants is named after the Greek physician, Pedianos Dioscorides, who wrote the herbal *De Materia Medica* in the first century AD. This herbal went on to influence other herbals, and so medical practice, for the next 1800 years. This tuber is an important crop throughout tropical America, the Caribbean, Africa and Asia. Among the 600 or so species in this group only a few are edible; some of the non-edible forms are very poisonous.

Description   Yams grow from underground tubers as a twining vine with shiny, dark green, heart-shaped leaves. Sometimes the leaves are tinged purple on the upper surface and are purple underneath. Yam tubers range in shape from small and round to large, irregular and elongated. As well as the tubers that form

underground, some yams form small tubers on the stems. These can be used to propagate new plants. *D. alata* is the species most commonly grown in Asia and the one most widely available in Australia. Its tubers have brown skin and white flesh. *D. batatas,* known as Chinese yam, is grown in parts of China and Japan. Tubers are more regular and elongated, like a carrot, but they are used in the same way as *D. alata*.

Cultivation   Yams are relatively easy to grow in the right climate. Plant when the tuber begins to sprout in early spring. If a whole tuber is not available then plant the top portion, which is the part that sprouts first. Plant the tuber a few centimetres below the surface of the soil, leave about 50 cm between plants and 1 m between

the growing season, but the soil must be well drained. They will thrive in sun or semishade. Grow them up a trellis or stake each plant. Tubers can be stored for two to three months. Yams will grow in cooler climates as long as they are started early in spring, and kept well watered during the hot dry months. *D. batatas* will tolerate much colder climates than *D. alata*.

Use Yams can be used in the same way as potatoes. The flavour is fairly bland with a floury, dry texture. Peel thickly first and then fry, boil, steam or bake. Always cut off any discoloured or damaged pieces. Tubers can also be cut into chips and fried. The Japanese dip pieces of yam in *tempura* batter and deep-fry. The tuber can also be grated and added to food to help bind it together, and can be added to soups to thicken them. Malaysians use the chopped tuber in desserts with coconut milk.

rows. In the tropics, stem and leaf growth continue right through the rainy season for about six months. New tubers begin to develop in late summer and autumn. When the vine dies back in late autumn the tubers are ready to harvest. Be careful when harvesting not to damage the thin skin. Plants need plenty of water during

Eleocharis dulcis Cyperaceae

water chestnut, Chinese water chestnut

ma tai (Ch); teki (In); ohkuru guai (Ja); moeum plong (Kh); hua heo (La); sengkuang (Ma); apulid (Ph); haeo chin, haew (Th); cu nang (Vi)

Water chestnuts are native to India, parts of South-East Asia and Polynesia. In some parts of Asia, water chestnuts are a dominant weed of rice fields and are harvested and grown as fodder for livestock. There is even one small sweet variety that is indigenous to northern Australia, and eaten by the Aboriginal people of that region. The forms now in cultivation come mainly from China where they have been grown for centuries and have been selected to increase size, sweetness and juiciness. Commercial crops are being grown in New South Wales, Northern Territory, Queensland and Victoria.

Description A sedge that typically grows on the edges of swamps and waterways, water chestnuts are perennial plants with narrow, tubular, upright leaves. Insignificant flowers form at the tips of the stems. Water chestnuts grow from spreading rhizomes that sucker and produce new plants during the growing season. In ideal conditions one corm can spread to cover as much as one square metre in a season. Leaves yellow and die back in autumn while at the same time chestnut corms form at the base of the plant.

Cultivation Grow water chestnuts in a pond or container that will hold water. An old bath is ideal, or a small plastic pool, or

line a trench in the vegetable garden with strong plastic. They like a reasonably rich soil with plenty of nutrients and a pH of 6.0 – 7.5. Give any added manure a couple of weeks to rot before the corms are planted. The soil needs to be about 30 cm deep. Plant corms about 30 cm apart, 4 cm below the surface of the soil with the growth buds at the top. Water well but do not flood. Corms should sprout about 10 days after planting as long as soil temperatures are above 13°C. When plants are growing strongly increase the water level to 10 – 20 cm above the soil. In cooler climates keep the water closer to 10 cm so it can warm up more quickly and so increase growth rates. These chestnuts grow most readily in warm to subtropical climates, although slightly cooler climates seem to produce sweeter corms. They need at least seven months of frost-free weather. The green tops grow best at daytime maximums of 30 – 35°C, while ideal temperatures for the corms to swell are 15 – 25°C. Corms begin to swell as the days get shorter in autumn. At the same time the stems above water begin to brown off and die. Harvest corms from winter to early spring; winter harvesting seems to produce the sweetest chestnuts. Corms keep well if left in the soil as long as the dead leaf tops are removed, soil temperatures stay below 13°C and there are no

heavy frosts. Birds love water chestnuts so it may be necessary to protect the crop from birds by temporarily covering with chicken wire.

After harvest, try planting azolla, a water fern that will fix nitrogen, thus lessening the need for fertiliser for the next crop; but azolla is a problem weed of waterways and ponds so make sure it doesn't escape to a nearby body of water. Water chestnuts will remove excess nutrients from fish ponds and decrease the growth of green algaes that take all the oxygen out of the water. Store water chestnuts in damp sand in a cool place if they need to be kept for any length of time. Never allow them to dry out. If they are to be eaten they can be stored in the refrigerator for several weeks or they can be frozen after blanching for four minutes.

Use Fresh water chestnuts must be peeled before use. Wash carefully, trim the top and the bottom and then remove the rest of the peel. These chestnuts can be eaten raw, either as they are, or added to salads. They are widely used in Asian cuisine in both savoury and sweet dishes, where they are valued for the sweet flavour and crisp, crunchy texture. Cooking actually improves the flavour. Water chestnuts are an important ingredient of many chop suey dishes and can be added to curries, soups and stir-fries. They are particularly good in vegetable stir-fries. A popular cooling drink is made by blending raw water chestnuts in water and adding sugar. Water chestnut flour is made by drying and grinding the corms. This is used to coat deep-fried food and to thicken sauces.

Elettaria cardamomum   Zingiberaceae

cardamom, Ceylon cardamom, Malabar cardamom

phalazee (Bu); sha jen (ChM); kapulaga (In); kravaan (Kh); ken ka wan (La); buah pelaga (Ma); luk grawan, luk kravan (Th)

This fragrant plant was known during medieval times in Europe as Grains of Paradise. Cardamom comes originally from India but has been widely grown through South-East Asia for more that 1000 years.

Description   Cardamom grows from creeping rhizomes with linear-lanceolate, strong, green leaves to about 3 m. The flowers are separate from the leaves and grow in spikes with white flowers that have a pink or mauve lip. Seed pods are very aromatic and green when fresh, but turn light brown when dried. They are oval and contain up to a dozen black seeds.

Cultivation Cardamoms like a nutrient-rich, well-drained soil with plenty of organic matter. Grow new plants from pieces of rhizome with one or more growth buds, plant these just below the surface of the soil and space about 60 cm apart. Cardamom grows naturally in the tropics and subtropics, where it does best in a sunny position. In cooler regions cardamom can be grown inside in a warm position, or in a heated greenhouse, during winter. Move back into a sheltered, warm position in spring and summer, but make sure it is protected from the hot afternoon sun. Feed with liquid seaweed fertiliser every couple of weeks during

spring and summer and ensure plants get plenty of water and frequent mist sprays. Each spring, mulch with some well-rotted manure. Pick pods while they are still green, and dry in the sun until they are pale green to brown.

Use Gently pound the dried pods so they are bruised, and add whole to curries or rice dishes. They can be dry roasted first to improve the flavour. It is not necessary to remove the seeds from the pods before using. In Thai cooking, cardamom pods are used in dishes influenced by Indian cuisine, like *Masaman curry*. Powdered cardamom seeds are also used in sweet dishes. In Thai and Indonesian cuisine, cardamom leaves are finely chopped and added to a number of dishes for their spicy

Cardamom pods with one pod broken open to show the seeds

flavour, and left whole they are used to wrap food before steaming or roasting. Young shoots can be steamed or roasted and eaten as a vegetable.

Elsholtzia ciliata Lamiaceae

Vietnamese balm

hsiang-ju (ChM); naginata-koju (Ja); phak luean (Th); rau kinh gioi, kin gioi ta (Vi)

This interesting plant is native to temperate China and Japan, and is now naturalised in parts of Europe.

Description Vietnamese balm is an annual that grows to about 1 m with bright green, pointed, serrated, ovate leaves. The stems are square with a deep red tinge. Pale purple flowers occur in autumn in long, one-sided flower heads.

The leaves have a sharp lemon-mint fragrance and a flavour that resembles lemon balm (*Melissa officinalis*) but is stronger.

Cultivation Grow from seed or cuttings taken in spring. In warm climates the stems will root in water. Sow seed into punnets and transplant to about 50 cm apart once seedlings are big enough to handle. Vietnamese balm likes most soils as long as they are well drained, and will grow in full sun or semishade. Top-dress with compost and manure, and water with seaweed fertiliser once a month or so during the growing season. Keep the flower heads cut back to encourage leaf growth.

Use Vietnamese balm leaves can be used in any recipe that calls for lemon balm, or with any food that will benefit from its tangy, lemon-mint flavour. It maintains its flavour well with cooking. In Vietnam, this herb is used in soups, noodle dishes and egg rolls. It is also added, finely chopped, to salads and salad dressing. It can be cooked and eaten as a vegetable on its own or added to other vegetables. Medicinally, a strong infusion can be used to treat coughs and colds.

Eryngium foetidum Apiaceae

culantro, eryngo, long-leafed coriander, stinkweed

chi rona (Kh); phak hom nhan (La); daun ketumbar jawa (Ma); phak chi doi, phak chee farang (Th); ngo gai (Vi)

This strong smelling herb comes originally from central and southern America where it has been used for centuries to add flavour to soups and stews. It has been grown in Europe since the early 17th century. Culantro is now popular in Asia and is often seen naturalised around rural villages. Its recent introduction is reflected in its name, the Thai name *phak chee farang* meaning 'foreign coriander', and the Vietnamese name *ngo gai* meaning 'thorny coriander'.

Description A low-growing herb to about 40 cm, culantro produces a rosette of stiff, dark green, elongated, toothed leaves. Strong stalks with toothed leaves grow from the centre of this, and these are topped by conical, pale green, tiny, pineapple-shaped flower heads. The

whole plant is strongly pungent with a scent and flavour resembling coriander (*Coriandrum sativum*).

Cultivation Culantro is a short-lived perennial that is treated as an annual in temperate regions. Grow from seed sown in punnets in winter or early spring, which can take several weeks to germinate. Plant seedlings out once they are big enough to handle easily. Space plants about 30 cm apart in all directions. This herb will grow in most soils as long as they are well drained, and likes a position in semishade or with morning sun, as very hot afternoon sun causes it to wilt. Culantro also grows well in pots, and this has the added advantage of being able to move the pot into the shade, or indoors in autumn to prolong the growing season. Remove the flower heads to encourage leaf growth, and feed once a month or so with seaweed fertiliser or fish emulsion. Snails and slugs love culantro, so be vigi-

lant in removing them or protect with a circle of ash or sawdust.

Use Leaves are eaten fresh and cooked in a range of dishes, especially those where the flavour of another ingredient needs to be disguised. Culantro is often used as a substitute for coriander, but unlike coriander it retains its flavour when dried. It is also sometimes substituted for garland chrysanthemum. Finely chopped leaves make an excellent garnish on all sorts of dishes, but in particular fish dishes. Stir chopped culantro into soups like Vietnamese beef and noodle or hot and sour fish soups, or add a whole leaf and remove before serving. Culantro is also used to flavour soups in Cambodia, while in Thailand and in Laos it is served fresh to accompany specially prepared fish and meat. It can also be added to steamed rice and tossed into mixed vegetables, curries and curry pastes. Culantro can be chopped and added to dips like hummus.

Etlingera elatior Zingiberaceae

torch ginger, Philippine waxflower

keong fa (ChC); jiang hua (ChM); combrang, honje (In); myoga (Ja); bunga kantan, bunga siantan (Ma); kaalaa (Th)

This ginger is native to Indonesia and New Guinea but is widely grown in tropical regions of the world because of its beautiful flowers.

Description Torch ginger is a large perennial plant with linear, lance-shaped leaves that can be 80 cm long. The leaves are dark green above and purple-green below. The whole plant can reach 6 m in height. In midsummer, flower stems to 1.5 m grow from the centre of the clump bearing a cone-shaped, deep pink flower head up to 30 cm long.

Cultivation Grow new plants by dividing old plants in spring or summer, or by planting fresh seed when soil temperatures are more than 20°C. Plant seeds in individual pots and keep them in a warm position. Space plants about 50 cm apart. The minimum night-time temperature this plant can tolerate without damage is 15°C, so in cooler climates grow it in a heated greenhouse. Torch ginger does best in a rich, composted soil, and likes full sun or semishade and plenty of water during the growing season.

Use Pick the flower while the bud is still tightly folded and eat either raw or cooked. The buds can be steamed or roasted, and are also added as a flavouring to curries and other spicy food because of their unusual tangy flavour. In Singapore and Malaysia, the buds are cut in half lengthways and added to fish curries, or sliced finely and sprinkled into salads. The Thais finely slice the flower heads and stir them into dips and salads, while the Japanese prepare them in the same way and use them as a garnish for sashimi and soups. The centre of the stem can be steamed and served with rice, while semi-ripe fruits are added to soups and stews, and ripe fruits used to make sweets.

Foeniculum vulgare   Apiaceae

fennel

samong-saba (Bu); adas pedas (In); jintan manis (Ma); yira (Th)

Fennel is native to the Mediterranean region and was used by the ancient Egyptians and early Romans. It was recommended by early Roman writers as an antidote for snakebite and attacks by mad dogs, as well as to give strength to athletes and soldiers. Fennel has also been used medicinally in Asia for many centuries, and is now naturalised in many parts of the world.

Description   Fennel is an extremely hardy perennial, which can be biennial or annual depending on climate, and is commonly found growing on wastelands. It can grow up to 2 m in height. It has strong, green flower stems and feathery, yellow-green leaves. The tiny, yellow flowers grow at the top of the plant in flat umbels and are followed by light brown, flat, ribbed seeds. There is a bronze form of fennel (*Foeniculum vulgare* 'Purpurascens') which grows to only 1 m and has attractive, red-bronze foliage; another form is Florence fennel (*Foeniculum vulgare* var. *dulce*) that develops a white bulbous base with flat, overlapping, celery-like stalks. It is smaller growing and usually regarded as an annual, but is otherwise similar to ordinary fennel.

Cultivation   Propagate all fennels from seed sown in spring. Sow seed where the plants are to grow and thin to about 40 cm between plants. Fennel will self-sow readily once established, and is a declared noxious weed in some regions. It grows best in full sun in a light, well-drained soil with some added compost and manure. Leaves are most succulent if plants are watered regularly, but fennel is drought tolerant and will endure long periods without water. Pick leaves at any time, and harvest seeds in autumn by cutting off the seed heads as the first seeds begin to turn brown. Hang them upside down inside paper bags in an airy dry position out of direct light. Once dry, strip the seeds from the seed heads and store in an airtight container.

Use   Fennel has numerous medicinal and culinary uses; the seeds, stems and leaves, as well as the bulbous base of Florence

74

fennel, are all edible with a delicious anise flavour and scent. This flavour means fennel combines particularly well with fish. In Asian cuisine, fennel seeds are added to spice and curry mixtures, especially those used with fish. They are also an ingredient of *garam masala*, which is a mixture of ground spices that is sprinkled over dishes at the end of cooking to enhance the flavour and fragrance. The seeds are an important ingredient of some pickles. In Malaysia, fennel is often combined with cumin in curry mixes.

Dry roasted fennel seeds are used as a breath freshener, handed around at the end of the meal, and for hundreds of years the seeds and leaves have been used in Asia to treat colic and other stomach upsets.

Glycine max Fabaceae

soybean, vegetable bean, vegetable soybean

tai tou, wong tau, hak tau (ChC); da dou, huang dou (yellow), hei dou (black), qing dou (green), mao dou (hairy) (ChM); kacang kedele (In); daizu (dried), eda mame (fresh) (Ja); kachang bulu rimau (Ma); utaw (Ph)

Soybeans are native to China and Japan, where they are cultivated as a food and fodder crop. They have been grown and eaten in China since 2000 BC, and are now cultivated in many Asian countries, where they are a valuable food source, second only to rice.

or mauve flowers are followed by hairy pods in groups of up to fifteen. They are carried on short stalks, and each pod contains about four seeds. Seeds are generally ovoid, and can be yellow, brown, grey and black. Hundreds of different varieties have been grown worldwide.

Description This annual bean grows to 30 – 80 cm in height, with hairy stems and green, trifoliate leaves. Small, white

Cultivation Soybeans can be grown in temperate, subtropical and tropical climates. It is important to select the right

75

variety for the right climate. They will grow in a wide range of soils as long as they are well drained. Sow seeds in early summer where they are to grow, 20 cm apart in rows that are 80 cm apart. Seeds will only germinate when soil temperatures are higher than 15°C. Side-dress with potassium nitrate when the plants begin flowering, to increase pod set and the number of beans in each pod. Water regularly once the plants begin to flower, as water stress will reduce the number of flowers and so the number of pods; conversely heavy rains and over watering reduce pollination and consequently pod set. Start harvesting green pods about 12 weeks from planting while the pods are still bright green and the beans are still plump. Harvest by picking individual pods or by pulling the whole plant and then removing the pods. Fully mature beans are harvested when the whole plant turns brown and begins to die — generally about a month after the green bean harvest stage. Dig up the whole plant, shake the dirt from the roots and hang to dry in a shady, airy position out of direct light. Once completely dry, remove the dried beans from the pods and store in airtight containers.

Photograph courtesy Digger's Seeds

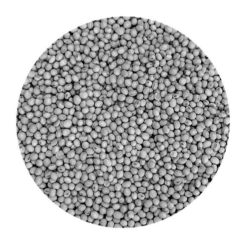

Use Soybean seeds have the highest protein content of all the cultivated legumes while containing little or no starch. They contain more protein by weight than red meat; also twice as much calcium as milk, and are high in vitamins A and B. It would be hard to imagine a more versatile food. Young pods with seeds are boiled for 10 – 15 minutes until the pods open and release the seeds. Discard the pods and eat the seeds in the same way as any other bean seed (broad beans or lima beans for example). Young plants and leaves can also be eaten as a vegetable. Mature seeds (beans) are dried and processed to produce bean curd, soya sauce, soya oil, soya milk, soya flour and textured vegetable protein. This protein is used as a substitute for meat in many vegetarian products. Fermented black soy beans are used to make black bean sauce. Dried mature seeds are also cooked as a vegetable and used in soups, salads and stews. They need to be soaked and cooked for a long time before they are soft enough to eat. Seeds can also be sprouted and used in salads and stir-fries or just eaten on their own.

Hemerocallis spp.   Hemerocallidaceae

day lily, dried lily buds, golden needles, golden vegetable

gum tsoy, gum jum (Ch); kaa chek (Kh); bunga pisang (Ma); dok mai jin (Th); kim cham (Vi)

Day lilies probably come originally from China, although they are now found growing wild from China to Europe. A day lily is depicted in a Chinese painting dating from the 12th century, and in that country it was formerly known as *hsuan t'sao* which translates as 'the plant of forgetfulness', as it was thought to cure sadness by causing memory loss.

Description   There are some 15 species of day lily and many hundreds of cultivars. The species traditionally used in China are *H. fulva* and *H. flava* but other day lilies can be used. Day lilies are perennials that grow from a creeping, tuberous root stock with linear, dark green leaves. Flowers grow on smooth stems to about 50 cm, and can be orange, yellow-orange or yellow, with many shades in between. Some modern cultivars have flowers in red, pink and purple shades. Flowers generally last for only one day.

Cultivation   Day lilies can be grown in tropical and temperate regions. Most lilies like full sun, although some will tolerate partial shade. They grow best in a fertile soil that is enriched with compost and manure in early spring. Grow by planting bare-rooted plants about 30 cm apart each way, in spring or autumn. They can also be grown from seed, but flower colour may not be true to the parent plant. Protect young plants from snails and slugs, but once fully developed, day lilies are tough, trouble free plants that need little care, and will happily naturalise in some positions. For more prolific flowering, lift, divide and replant every three years. Harvest day lily buds the day before they burst into flower, when they should be delightfully fragrant and crunchy.

Use Day lilies are best known for their edible flowers that are highly prized in Chinese and Japanese cooking. The buds are eaten fresh and dried, and used for their musky flavour in a range of Chinese dishes. Soak dried buds in water before using. Add to salads, soups, stir-fries and meat and noodle dishes. The Japanese dip them in *tempura* batter and deep-fry. Young shoots are eaten as a vegetable — steamed, boiled or fried — while bulbs are boiled, baked, mashed and eaten too.

Hibiscus sabdariffa Malvaceae

rosella, roselle, Florida cranberry, Jamaica sorrel, red sorrel, Queensland jelly plant

asam susur (Ma); krachiap daeng (Th)

This distinctive plant is native to tropical Asia and Africa and is now widely cultivated in tropical regions of the world.

Description An attractive annual shrub, rosella grows upright to about 2 m with magenta-red stems, large, flat, lobed, green leaves and delicate yellow flowers with deep red centres. The most striking parts of the plant are the fleshy bright magenta-red calyces (the calyx is the outermost layer of petals) that grow around the seed pods in late autumn and winter. Harvest calyces when they are about 2 – 3 cm long.

Cultivation Rosella grows in tropical climates and needs a long growing season to flower and then produce the fleshy calyces. Plants will only flower when daylight hours go below 11 hours in autumn, so in cooler regions grow from seed sown inside in early spring. In warmer regions grow from seed sown, or cuttings taken, at the beginning of the rainy season. Place seeds or seedlings about 2 cm deep and 30 – 40 cm apart, with about 1 m between rows. Rosella grows in most soils as long as they are well drained. It needs full

sun, and is relatively drought-tolerant although frost-sensitive. Feed regularly during the growing season.

Use Rosella's bright red calyces are the part eaten. They have a sharp, acid flavour and are high in vitamin C. They can be made into an infusion by pouring boiling water over the calyces. This can be drunk hot or left to stand until cool, sweetened to taste, and ice added to make a delicious summer drink. In South-East Asia, infusions of rosella are used to add flavour to curries. Also young shoots are added to sour soups, curries and stews, and young leaves are added to salads or steamed and eaten as a vegetable. The calyces are also used to make sauces, jams and jellies.

Houttuynia cordata Saururaceae

fish plant, fish-cheek mint

ji cai (Ch); dokudami (Ja); hi trey (Kh); phak khao tong (La); phak khao tong (Th), rau diep ca, giap ca (Vi)

This plant is a decorative ground cover already grown in many gardens. It is native to South-East Asia and China and is often served with fish, hence its common names.

Description Fish plant is a low, spreading plant with leaves that are pointed and heart-shaped, and which can range in colour from green to cream, pink, yellow, red and blue-green in various combina-

tions on different cultivars. The flowers are made up of white bracts (modified leaves) with a bright yellow centre spike. The whole plant forms a dense mat and can become invasive.

Cultivation This spreading herb is best grown by dividing old plants in autumn or spring. Plant in a semishaded position in any reasonable soil, although it does best in damp soil or near a pond. Keep well

regions the whole plant dies back in winter to reappear in spring.

Use Fish plant leaves are strongly flavoured, with a unique pungency. In Vietnam and Cambodia they are used as one of the herbs and salad leaves that are wrapped, in varying combinations, in rice paper, dipped in sauces and eaten during the course of the meal. Leaves are also added to salads and used as a fresh garnish for egg dishes, as well as dishes made from strongly flavoured meat and fish. In China, fish plant is used medicinally to treat rashes. In Japan, it is used to treat insect bites while the Vietnamese eat it to relieve haemorrhoids and stomach cramps.

watered during dry weather. Space plants about 30 cm apart. Fish plant makes a good pot plant and will grow well in a hanging basket where it will hang over the side. It grows equally well in tropical and temperate climates although in cold

Ipomoea aquatica Convolvulaceae

water spinach, swamp cabbage, kangcong, ipomea, water convolvulus

ung tsoi, ung-choi, tung tsoi, kang kong (ChC); eng-chai (ChH); kong xin cai, weng cai (ChM); kangkung (In); asagaona (Ja); trakoun (Kh); phak bung (La); kangkung (Ma); kangkong (Ph); phak bung (Th); rau muong (Vi)

This plant probably comes originally from India and is now widely grown through most of Asia and some parts of Africa.

Description Water spinach is a perennial with narrow, spear-shaped leaves and hollow stems. In cold climates it should be treated as an annual. The stems trail across the ground and send out roots at each of the nodes. Large white or pink flowers open in autumn. There seem to be two varieties — one that thrives in water, and one that will tolerate being grown in the garden as long as it is not allowed to dry out.

Cultivation Grow from seed sown from spring to autumn, or cuttings taken in spring or summer. Seeds and seedlings need daytime maximums above 25°C before they will germinate and thrive. Plant out into nutrient-rich soil that is permanently wet if possible, spacing plants about 15 cm apart, in sun or semi-shade. This plant grows best in the tropics, but can be grown in the warmer months in temperate regions if plants are kept constantly moist. Whole plants are ready to harvest about 45 days after planting, but leaves can be harvested as soon as the plants are large enough. In Japan and China, plants are sometimes grown in fish ponds because the fish like to feed on them.

Use Cook young shoots and leaves as a vegetable. Always use the leaves and stems as fresh as possible. As water spinach reduces dramatically in bulk once cooked, make sure there is plenty to start with. Plants are high in protein, fibre and iron, and are sometimes fed to people with anaemia. Leaves are delicious stir-fried with shrimp, garlic and ginger, with the water spinach only being added two minutes before serving. Vietnamese cooks value this vegetable for its crunchy stems and limp leaves, they use it in stir-fries and soups. Finely shredded stems are also added to salads. Leaves and stems can be pickled too. The leaves have mild laxative properties.

Ipomoea batatas Convolvulaceae

sweet potato

fun-shu (ChC); hun-chi (ChH); fan shu (ChM); ubi-keledek, ubi jalar, ubi manis (In); satsuma imo (Ja); keledek (Ma); camotes (Ph)

These potatoes came originally from central America but are now widely grown in tropical regions of the world. They were introduced to Europe at the beginning of the 16th century but didn't find their way to China until the end of the same century. They are the seventh most popular food crop in the world.

Description Sweet potato is a perennial plant that is usually grown as an annual. It grows from underground tuberous roots with trailing, twisting stems that can be 6 m long. Leaves are fairly variable but are generally heart-shaped. Roots grow from stem nodes as they touch the ground, and most of these grow into more tubers. Up to eight tubers can be produced on each plant. The flesh of the tubers can be white, yellow, purple, red, orange and brown. White-fleshed varieties tend to be less sweet than the others.

Cultivation Sweet potatoes can be grown from seeds, cuttings or by planting tubers. They do best in full sun in a fertile, open, sandy soil with some added manure and compost. If the soil is too wet or heavy then the roots tend to be long and stringy instead of short and plump. Grow them in mounds about 30 cm high, and plant each tuber about 1 m from the next. Keep free from weeds and don't give too much nitrogen or there will be leaf growth at the expense of tuber growth. They benefit from regular additions of potash. Sweet potatoes usually need four to five frost-free months in order to produce tubers of a reasonable size, although there are some cultivars that will produce tubers in as little as three months. Sweet potatoes are regarded as a tropical crop, but they can be grown in the summer in temperate regions.

Tubers are ready to harvest when the leaves begin to yellow, and when a small cut on the surface of the tuber does not turn yellow. Harvest all the tubers at once, brush clean and store. Sweet potato tubers can be stored for up to four months as long as the air temperature is about 10°C. Alternatively harvest the tubers as they are needed and only complete the har-

vesting before the first frost. Store some tubers for replanting.

Use Sweet potato tubers can be boiled, baked, fried or made into flour, starch or cereal. In Japan, they are also made into noodles, cakes and breads. In many other Asian countries, they are made into sweet foods like pies, puddings, biscuits, cakes and desserts. They are also used to make alcoholic drinks. Young leaves and the tips of the vines can be washed and boiled and eaten as a vegetable. Alternatively, add young sweet potato leaves to chillies and prawns for a quick, delicious stir-fry. Leaves and stems are high in protein and vitamin C. All parts of the sweet potato plant can be used as stock feed; the tubers are usually cooked before being fed to pigs.

Kaempferia sp.   Zingiberaceae

K. galanga kenkur, lesser galangal
K. rotunda resurrection lily

kenkur, kentjoer (In); prah (Kh); houa ka xai (La); cekur (Ma); proh hom (Th)

There are about 50 species of *Kaempferia*, many of which are grown in tropical regions for their decorative leaves and flowers. A few are also grown for their spicy tuberous roots.

Description   Resurrection lily is a low-growing, spreading plant with rounded leaves that are silver-green above and purple beneath. Leaves are more upright than flat. Flowers are purple and white. The white or yellow rhizome has a camphory, earthy scent and flavour. A closely related species that also has an edible rhizome is *K. galanga*. This grows with rounded, green leaves that sometimes have red markings; the underneath is paler than the top. Leaves usually lie flat on the ground. Flowers are fragrant, white and mottled purple.

Cultivation   Grow new plants from pieces of root with one or two buds. Plant these in autumn or spring about 5 cm deep and 40 cm apart. These plants are tropical but can be grown in more temperate regions inside or in a greenhouse. The rhizome will grow more quickly if the planting area is covered in clear plastic to maintain warmth and humidity. Remove the plastic once shoots appear. Water frequently and mist regularly in hot weather. Leave fairly dry during winter, when the tubers are dormant. In tropical regions, these plants are usually grown in areas with more than 1000 mm of rainfall a year. They like a fertile, open, loamy soil that is well drained because they do not like to be waterlogged. The rhizomes are harvested in autumn.

Use   The rhizome and tuberous roots are often pounded and added to a range of dishes. In Thai cuisine both the roots and leaves are used, especially in curry paste for fish, and the young leaves eaten raw as a vegetable. In Malaysia, leaves are finely sliced and added in small amounts to sal-

ads. These rhizomes are particularly popular in Bali, and are an essential ingredient of Indonesian peanut sauce. The rhizomes are also used medicinally. In Thailand, the crushed roots are combined with whisky as a headache cure.

Lablab purpureus Fabaceae

hyacinth bean, Egyptian bean, Indian bean, bonavist bean, Chinese flowering bean, dolichos bean

bian dou, rou dou, que dou (ChM); pin tau, tseuk tau (ChC); kerara (In); fujimame (Ja); kakcang kara, kachang sepat (M); tua nang, tua pep (Th)

This bean is extensively grown in tropical South-East Asia, India, China and northern Africa. It probably comes originally from India but was introduced to the other countries in ancient times. The botanical name 'lablab' comes from an Arabic word that describes the dull rattle that the beans make in the dry shell.

Purple hyacinth bean

Description This is a very vigorous perennial bean with climbing and bush forms. In cold regions it is grown as an annual. There are several varieties with varying leaf and flower colour. Leaves consist of three dark green or red-purple, rounded leaflets, and flowers can be white, pink or purple and are fragrant, occurring in racemes in summer and autumn. These flowers are followed by green or purple curved, flattened pods with wavy margins that contain three to five seeds. This bean is often grown as an ornamental vine because of its attractive foliage and flowers.

Cultivation In the tropics, hyacinth beans are planted in late spring and summer, and produce beans by late autumn and again the following spring. In temperate regions, grow this bean from seed sown in spring and harvest pods about four months later. Sow seed about 2 cm deep and 30 cm apart. Hyacinth beans like full sun and a reasonably fertile, well-drained soil. Bean production is more prolific if vines are trained up a fence, trellis or tripod. Keep well-watered during dry weather.

Use Dried bean seeds, young leaves and the swollen root can all be eaten. Immature pods and beans are boiled and eaten as a vegetable, and are also added to curries. In Malaysia, these beans are the favourite bean pod to add to curries. In China and India, ripe seeds are used as a pulse. They are also sprouted. These beans are never eaten raw as they contain a poisonous substance that is destroyed with cooking. Being a legume, hyacinth beans are often planted as a cover crop to improve soil fertility and stop erosion. They are also a good fodder crop.

Lactuca sativa var. *asparagina*   Asteraceae

stem lettuce, asparagus lettuce, celtuce, Chinese lettuce

ngau lei shaang tsoi, woo chu, woh sun (ChC); wo sun, wo ju sun, jing wo ju (ChM); stemuretasu, kaki-jisha (Ja)

All lettuces come originally from the area now known as Asia Minor, Iran and Turkestan. Lettuces have been used for food and medicine for more than 6000 years. Stem lettuce probably comes originally from China, where it is still widely grown.

Description Stem lettuce, as indicated by its name, is grown for its elongated flower stem. It starts as a typical lettuce with a loose cluster of light green leaves. From this grows a central stalk with tiny leaves at the top. This stem elongates and can reach more than 1 m in height, but it is usually harvested before this.

Young plant with the stem beginning to elongate

85

Cultivation Stem lettuce can be grown in a range of climates. It will tolerate mild frosts, but seed will not germinate in very hot weather. In temperate regions grow it from seed sown in autumn, winter or spring. Space plants about 30 cm apart. In the tropics, grow from seed sown in autumn. Stem lettuce likes full sun, a fertile soil that is well drained and regular water. Harvest the stem when it is 30 – 40 cm long and at least 2 cm across. This usually takes about 100 days. Cut it just above the basal leaves.

Use Stems need to be peeled before use, as this outer layer contains a bitter sap. Once the outer layer has been removed only the pale green, soft core is left. This can be diced or sliced and eaten fresh or cooked by boiling, braising, stir-frying or stewing. The stem has a subtle, cucumber-lettuce flavour and a crisp texture, and is regarded as a delicacy in China and some other Asian countries.

Lagenaria siceraria   Cucurbitaceae

edible bottle gourd, bottle gourd, calabash, dudi, New Guinea bean, white flowered gourd

wu lo kwa, poo kwa (ChC); peh poh (ChH); mao gua, hu lu gua (ChM); labu air (Ma); bau (Vi)

Bottle gourd remains have been found in Egyptian tombs more than 4000 years old, and in Mexican archaeological sites dating back to 7000 BC. They probably come originally from tropical Africa. As gourds have been shown to float and still remain viable, it is possible that they originally reached Asia from Africa by floating on ocean currents.

Description These vigorous, annual, climbing gourds have ribbed stems and large heart-shaped leaves. The single white flowers grow in the axils of the leaves and usually open in the evenings. Fruits vary from club-shaped and bottle-shaped to round, with numerous varia-

Club shaped gourds, sometimes called New Guinea Bean (photograph courtesy Digger's Seeds)

tions in between, but they generally have pale green skin with mottled white patches. Some gourds, especially the rounded ones, are too bitter to eat even when young. The edible bottle gourds most commonly seen for sale in Australia are long, round in cross-section and often slightly club-shaped.

Cultivation Grow from seed sown from late spring to early summer in cool regions, and late winter to autumn in the tropics. If the seed is soaked for 12 hours first it usually germinates more rapidly. Sow seed in groups of three where they are to grow, leaving about 1 m between plants. Thin to the strongest seedling. These plants will not tolerate frosts and do well in regions with warm, wet summers. They will grow in temperate regions but need to be kept well watered. In these regions, flowers will sometimes need to be hand pollinated for fruit to set. Even if fruit sets it may not fully mature. Edible bottle gourds like a fertile, well-composted soil and full sun. They need some support or trellis and, if allowed, will grow over trees and shrubs and may smother them. Nip out the terminal growing shoot to encourage more lateral shoots. Large gourds may need to be supported by being enclosed in a string bag tied to the trellis, or else the weight of the fruit will pull the vine down. Young fruit can be harvested once they are 10 cm long. Older fruit from some forms are still edible and are used in soups. These can be harvested at any time. Gourds being harvested for their hard shell should be left on the vine until it dies back in autumn.

Use Young fruits, 10 – 20 cm long, are eaten as vegetables and added to curries, especially in Malaysia and Vietnam. The flesh is firm and white. In Vietnam, they are also added to soup, stir-fried with pork or chicken, and fried together with eggs. In Japan, dried strips of gourd flesh are used in sushi, and to tie small packets of food. Mature fruits develop a hard, woody shell when dried, and they have been used as water carriers, cups, bowls, floats and even as musical instruments. Medicinally the skins have been used to treat diarrhoea.

Limnophila aromatica Scrophulariaceae

rice paddy herb, swamp plant, swamp leaf

phak khayaeng (Th); ngo om, rau om (Vi)

Rice paddy herb is indigenous to Australia, India and southern Asia and often grows as a weed in rice fields.

Description This semi-aquatic herb grows to about 30 cm with trailing, succulent stems. It has small, linear leaves with serrated edges that grow in groups of three around the stems. Pale blue and cream flowers grow at the ends of the stems.

Cultivation Rice paddy herb can be grown in any good, moist soil in full sun or semi-shade. It likes added compost, and mulching helps to keep the soil moist. Alternatively, plant it at the edge of a

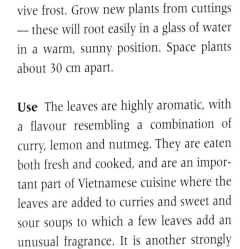

pond or grow it in a pot that sits in another container that is topped up regularly with fresh water. In cooler regions this pot can be moved indoors in winter to help it survive very cold weather, as it won't survive frost. Grow new plants from cuttings — these will root easily in a glass of water in a warm, sunny position. Space plants about 30 cm apart.

Use The leaves are highly aromatic, with a flavour resembling a combination of curry, lemon and nutmeg. They are eaten both fresh and cooked, and are an important part of Vietnamese cuisine where the leaves are added to curries and sweet and sour soups to which a few leaves add an unusual fragrance. It is another strongly flavoured herb that is used to disguise the taste of some strongly flavoured meats and fish. Rice paddy herb is also delicious with roasted vegetables and any chicken dish.

Luffa acutangula Cucurbitaceae

angled luffa, angled loofah, Chinese okra

sze kwa (ChC); si gua, lin jiao si gua, you lin si gua (ChM); petola, gambas, ketola manis (In); hechima (Ja); ketola segi (Ma); patola (Ph); buab (Th); muop khia (Vi)

Angled luffas come originally from north-western India but are now widely spread through South-East Asia. Luffas are grown commercially in New South Wales, Northern Territory and Queensland.

Description Luffas are vigorous vines with hairy stems and branching tendrils. The large, rough, lobed leaves are ovate, while the male and female flowers are yellow, with female flowers occurring singly and male flowers in groups. Fruits are elongated and cylindrical in shape, with ten strong ribs. Seeds are light brown to black and crinkled. Luffas are day-length sensitive. Short-day, long-day and day-neutral cultivars exist.

Cultivation In temperate regions, luffas are sown in spring and summer; in sub-tropical regions, from spring to autumn, and in the tropics, from autumn to early winter. Soak seeds in water for 24 hours before planting. Sow seed either into raised mounds or flat ground about 50 cm apart. Plants grow best when trained up a trellis about 2 m high. Start training plants around the trellis when seedlings are about 15 cm high. Heavy rain can damage the flowers and fruit. Plants are frost-sensitive, and cold weather may cause young fruit to drop off the plant. Luffas do best in well-drained, sandy soils

that are rich in organic matter, with a pH of 5.5 to 7.0. They generally take 90 days from planting to first harvest. Fertilise with a high-nitrogen fertiliser before planting, and then again after about five weeks. Water regularly during dry weather. Flowering should start about eight weeks after germination, and pruning lateral shoots will increase the number of female flowers and so the number of fruit. Try hand pollination if fruit are not setting. Begin harvesting fruit once they are 10 cm long. If the fruits are allowed to get too big they become fibrous and start to produce chemicals that can cause

diarrhoea. Angled luffas will produce about 20 fruit per plant.

Use To prepare the fruit, wash well and use a peeler or sharp knife to take the sharp edges off the ridges. Young luffas are sliced and eaten raw in salads, or cooked as a vegetable by boiling, frying, steaming or braising. They are also added to soups and stir-fries with other vegetables. Their mild, slightly bitter flavour combines well with fresh herbs, with coconut milk, and in particular with vegetable curries. In China, slices of luffa are dried in the sun and stored. They are later added to soups. Fruits will keep in the refrigerator for a few weeks as long as they are not too cold. Young leaves and flower buds can be eaten cooked as a vegetable on their own, or combined with other vegetables in a stir-fry. Fully mature seeds are roasted, sprinkled with salt, and served as a snack in the same way as pumpkin seeds.

Luffa cylindrica Cucurbitaceae

smooth luffa, dish rag gourd, dishcloth gourd, sponge gourd, vegetable sponge

seui kwa, see kwa (ChC); si gua, shui gwa, pu tong si gua, man gua (ChM); hechima, ito-uri (Ja); belustra, loang (In); petola manis, petola bulat (Ma); loofah, patola (Ph); buop horm (Th); muop huong (Vi)

Smooth luffas originated in north-western India but are now widely grown throughout South-East Asia and in many other tropical regions of the world.

Description The smooth luffa fruit has no ribs and is usually larger, but is otherwise similar to angled luffa (see page 89).

Cultivation Smooth luffas are grown in the same way as angled luffas except that the fruit are usually left to fully mature. This generally takes four to five months from planting. The fruit are then treated and the internal skeleton used as a sponge.

Use Young fruit can be eaten. Usually, however, mature fruit are used for their sponge like skeleton. To remove the flesh, place fruit into hot water and leave for 24 hours. Then repeat each day until all the flesh and skin has rotted away leaving the fibrous skeleton. Once this skeleton (or sponge) is dry it will keep indefinitely. The spongy skeleton can be used as a bath sponge, as well as for cleaning glassware, utensils and dishes. Sponges are also used to stuff cushions and mattresses. The bitter juice from the fruit is an ingredient in Chinese medicine.

Sponge (photograph courtesy Digger's Seeds)

Lycium barbarum Solanaceae

Chinese boxthorn, common boxthorn, Chinese matrimony vine, tea tree, wolf berry

kau kei, kou kay choi (ChC); gou qi (ChM); kuko (Ja); kau ky (Vi)

This plant is native to China and Japan, and can now be found growing in the warmer, but not tropical, regions of the world, especially Europe. Some taxonomists suggest that the various forms of Chinese boxthorn actually belong to three different species (*L. barbarum*, *L. chinense* and *L. europaeum*), while others maintain that they are all different forms of *L. barbarum*.

Description Chinese boxthorn grows as a small tree of about 2 m with long arching branches. It has mid to dark green, ovate leaves and mauve flowers. These are followed by small, elongated, orange or red berries. Most forms have thorns but some do not.

Cultivation This plant grows easily from seed and has become a weed of waste ground in many regions of the world, growing from berries dropped by birds. Sow seed in spring in any well-drained soil in full sun. It can also be grown from cuttings taken in autumn or spring. Rootstocks will sucker, so don't grow it near any precious plants. If cut regularly and planted about 1 m apart, Chinese boxthorn makes a useful, dense, impene-

two or three times a year. Harvest berries in autumn, and leaves any time of the year.

Use Leaves are slightly bitter and are used fresh or dried as a flavouring, added to pork dishes and a range of soups. They can also be added to rice while it is cooking to give the rice a pleasant aromatic flavour. The small berries have a sweet anise flavour and are high in carotene. In China, they are added to important ceremonial dishes, especially those with chicken or duck. The berries are sold dried, in markets, and both the leaves and berries are made into a tea. They are regarded as being a tonic.

trable hedge, particularly if the thorny types are used. They need to be cut back

Manihot esculenta Euphorbiaceae

cassava, yuca, manioc, tapioca

mok shu (ChC); chew chi (ChH); mu shu (ChM); katela bodin (In); imanoka (Ja); ubi kayu, ubi tanah (Ma); kamoteng kahoy (Ph); mun sumpalung (Th); bosan hot (Vi)

Cassava comes originally from southern America but is now widely grown in most tropical regions of the world, where it is a staple food and an important source of carbohydrate.

Description This small short-lived perennial tree can grow to 5 m. It has smooth, reddish stems and large, bright green, lobed leaves, all of which contain a white latex substance. Male and female flowers grow in racemes from the leaf axils. Root tubers come in different shapes and sizes, but they are usually elongated, cylindrical and taper at each end. Each plant produces up to 10 tubers. There are many different cultivars, with varying tuber size and colour, and leaves of differing sizes.

Cultivation Grow new plants from cuttings and plant in full sun at least 1 m apart in all directions. Cassava can tolerate relatively dry conditions, light frosts and poor soil, but the soil must be well drained. It will grow in tropical, subtropical and mild temperate regions. Trees may reshoot from the ground after a heavy frost. Tubers take at least eight months to reach a reasonable size but last well when left in the ground, so in times of food shortage cassava can be a very important crop. Once harvested, the tubers will only stay fresh for a few weeks. Soils need plenty of added manure, once tubers have been dug, before anything else can be planted in the same position.

Use Both the edible root tubers and the very young leaves are eaten. Tubers are rich in carbohydrates. Tubers of the original forms of cassava were quite poison-

(photograph by H.F. Chin)

ous, containing hydrocyanic acid, and needed careful treatment (washing, peeling and boiling) before eating. Modern, sweet cultivars have very little or no poisons in them and any poisons present are found mostly in the skin. Peel the tubers and then boil, fry or bake before eating. They can be used to make chips. Tubers can also be made into flour that is then used to make cakes. Starch from the tubers is refined and sold as tapioca, and this is used as a thickener in a range of dishes. The tubers are low in protein so need to be supplemented by other foods higher in protein. Both the leaves and young shoots can also be eaten, but these must be cooked first, preferably boiled in water with the water then discarded. Use cooked leaves in salads or just eat as a vegetable. They are also used to wrap food before steaming, grilling or baking. Leaves are high in calcium and vitamins A and C. Starch made from the tubers is used in the manufacture of paper and in laundries.

Mentha spp.   Lamiaceae

mints

heung fa choi (ChC); xiang hua cai (ChM); merdinah, kresnan, pudina (In); chi mahao, pak hom ho (Kh); phak horm (La); daun pudina, pohok (Ma); bai sarana (Th); rau thom, rau hung lui (Vi)

The mint family is extremely varied and it is often difficult to identify individual species because of their tendency to hybridise. There is also confusion with both common and scientific names. The mints most commonly used in Asian cuisine have a definite spearmint flavour, and so are probably cultivars and varieties of *M. arvensis*, corn mint, and *M. spicata*, spearmint.

Description Spearmint grows to 60 cm with long, bright green leaves which are serrated and lanceolate. Pinkish flowers grow in terminal spikes. Corn mint has hairy stems and leaves, and pink or white flowers. *M. arvensis* var. *piperascens* is known as Japanese mint and has more rounded leaves with some reddish markings. All mints spread by underground runners.

Cultivation These mints can be grown from seed, by taking cuttings or by dividing clumps. Sow seed in spring and prick out seedlings into individual pots when they are large enough to handle. Plant into the garden in summer. The average family needs only one or two plants. Mints hybridise readily, so seed often doesn't grow true to the parent plant. Consequently, if a mint with a particular flavour is needed, it is much better to grow it from cuttings or by root division. Take cuttings of non-flowering growth in spring or summer; divide plants at any time. Any piece that has some root growth will produce a new plant. Mints will grow in most soils as long as they are not too dry; they even tolerate heavy clay. They grow in sun or semishade. Most mints spread aggressively so to stop them taking over the garden, plant into a container or into an individual bed.

Use Use spearmint to make mint tea, fruit punches, apple jellies and fresh chutneys. Mint is an essential ingredient of many Middle Eastern dishes, but is restricted to only a few of the traditional

Spearmint

cuisines in Asia, namely Cambodian, Laotian, Malaysian, Thai and Vietnamese. The leaves are used in salads and curries in Malaysia, in salads in Cambodia and Vietnam, and also in salads and as a garnish and in green curry sauces in Thailand. Mint is also used medicinally, and fresh and dried leaves are sold in Chinese pharmacies.

Momordica charantia Cucurbitaceae

bitter melon, bitter cucumber, bitter gourd, karella, balsam pear, alligator pear

fu kwa, pava-aki (ChC); kor-kuey (ChH); ku gua, jin li zhi, lao pu tao (ChM); pare, peria (In); reishi, niga uri (Ja); peria (Ma); ampalaya (Ph); ma ra (Th); muop dang, kha qua (Vi)

Bitter melons are cultivated in tropical regions all over the world, including the Caribbean, China, India and South-East Asia. They are grown commercially in New South Wales, Northern Territory, Queensland and Victoria.

Description Bitter melon plants are vigorous climbing vines with slender, five-angled stems. The large, lobed leaves can be 18 cm in diameter, and the male and female flowers are yellow and solitary. The unusual fruit are warty in appearance and hang down. They start off being pale green, then dark green and become yellow or orange when very ripe. When mature, the fruit splits into three sections that curve backwards to reveal numerous seeds enclosed in bright red coats or arils. The shape of the fruit can vary from long and tapering to pear-shaped. Varieties of bitter melon grown in Australia include 'Sta Rita' and 'Makiling' (both open pollinated), and their F1 hybrids 'Jade Star A' and 'Jade Star B'.

Cultivation These melons will grow in either tropical or subtropical climates. They grow best where night-time minimum temperatures are 20 – 25°C, but will tolerate minimums down to 18°C, particularly in the early stages of growth. Bitter melons do best in well-drained, light, sandy loams with plenty of organic matter, and a pH around 6.5, but will tolerate

that the melons can hang down away from the leaves. Remove some lateral shoots to prevent overcrowding. Water well during dry weather but don't over-water. The first flowers appear after about 50 days, and hand pollination may be necessary if there are not many bees around. Fruit should be pale green, thick and juicy when harvested, and it general-ly takes two to three weeks after fruit set to reach this stage. In good conditions melons will continue to be produced for up to six months.

a range of other soils. Plants grow well if they are sown in raised beds or ridges. This is especially important if the drainage is suspect. Add manure to the soil about three weeks before planting, and as long as there is plenty of organic matter in the soil, plants should not need to be fed again. Seeds need to be very fresh as they lose their viability quickly. They normally take five to ten days to germinate at soil temperatures of about 23°C. To increase the chances of germination, soak the seeds on damp paper towel for 24 hours, then wrap them in fresh damp paper towel and place into a plastic bag or jar and keep at a constant temperature of about 27°C for two days. By this time they should have germinated. Plant the seeds into individual pots, and keep in a warm place so that they are ready to be planted out, about 50 cm apart, once the weather is warm enough. This is in late spring to early summer in temperate regions, early spring in subtropical regions, and autumn to winter in the tropics. Protect from wind chill and too much sun. For good crop-ping, bitter melons need to be grown on a trellis about 2 m high. Ideally the trellis should then extend across as a 'roof' so

Use Bitter melon is so called because of its bitter flavour, and the darker the skin colour the more bitter the flavour. It is something of an acquired taste which enhances the flavour of other ingredients. Before eating bitter melon, peel, cut in half and remove the seeds. Use fresh in salads, cook it stuffed with rice and pork, shallow-fry thin slices or simply boil. Add slices to beef and black-bean sauce stir-fry, or chicken and mushrooms, or to veg-etable curries. Bitter melon can also be pickled and young leaves and shoots can be eaten. Always choose slender, apple green gourds. If they are yellow or too plump then they are probably over-ripe. If they are too bitter, then blanch first by slicing in half lengthwise, removing seeds and dropping the melon into sugared boil-ing water. Leave for a minute, remove and drain. Alternatively, parboil in salted water, drain well and rinse, or rub cut slices with salt, leave for ten minutes and then rinse well. The Chinese regard bitter melons as a tonic vegetable, but don't eat the seed as they are strongly purgative.

Moringa oleifera Moringaceae

horseradish tree, drumstick

sai jar (In); kacang kelor, kelur, buah keloh (Ma); mulunggay (Ph); chum ngay (Vi)

This tree grows wild in northern India, and was recorded in early writings as a medicinal plant. It was also depicted in tombs in Ancient Egypt, so it is not clear where it comes from originally. An oil extracted from the horseradish tree, and known as ben oil, was used by the Egyptians in religious ceremonies.

Description These small trees grow to about 8 m and make an ornamental street tree in tropical regions. They have tuberous roots and fern-like leaves. Decorative, pale yellow or cream flowers occur all year round, and are followed by long (to 30 cm), green pods covered by fine hairs. Pods turn brown when fully mature. The whole tree has a pungent scent and flavour.

Cultivation Grow horseradish tree from stem cuttings or seeds. It will tolerate dry conditions and survives in arid regions of the world. This tree is frost-tender and a severe frost can knock it back to ground level, but it will often reshoot. While a fully grown tree may be as high as 8 m, they are often straggly and need to be pruned heavily in autumn to encourage dense growth and keep the tree small. This will also make the leaves easier to harvest. In ideal conditions (warm wet summers and dry warm winters) trees may grow as much as 3 m in the first year,

and will often flower and fruit in the first year too. Pod production seems to increase if trees are water stressed. In cooler regions, start the tree in a pot, and stand it in a warm, sunny, sheltered corner during its first winter. The following spring, plant it out into a warm corner of the garden, near a north- or west-facing wall where it will get reflected heat.

Use A very nutritious tree, the leaves, roots, flowers and young shoots and pods are all eaten. Strip the leaflets from the

97

stem or pick young growing tips and cook as a vegetable by boiling or steaming. They have a pleasant mustardy flavour. Alternatively, add to curries, soups or rice. Young pods are scraped to remove the tough skin and then cooked and eaten like asparagus, or sliced into pieces and boiled. Flowers have a subtle radish flavour and can be eaten raw or used as a garnish. Europeans in Asia found that the roots of this tree made a good substitute for horseradish (*Armoracia rusticana*), so roots of young plants (about 1 m tall) can be peeled and then grated and blended with vinegar. Be careful to remove all the skin as it is poisonous. In India, dried and crushed seeds are used to purify water. Oil extracted from the tree is used in perfumery and gum from the bark is used as a thickening and emulsifying agent.

Murraya koenigii   Rutaceae

curry tree, Indian curry tree

pyin daw thein (Bu); daun kari (In); khi be (La); daun kari (Ma); bai kari (Th)

This small tree is a native of India and has been carried to different parts of the world by Indian immigrants. It is now widely grown in tropical regions of the world and can be found growing wild in some of these regions too.

Description   This small evergreen tree can reach 6 m under ideal conditions, but it is usually smaller. It has shiny, dark green, lance-shaped leaves with a drooping habit that grow alternately, with about 16 to each stem. The numerous, small, white flowers occur in clusters and are followed by green berries that turn purple-black when ripe. Trees often send up numerous suckers around the base.

Cultivation   Curry trees are tropical plants that grow easily from seeds, and new seedlings will often sprout under

existing trees. In regions where summers are hot and winters cold, curry trees need to be grown in pots and moved to a semi-shaded position in summer, then into a greenhouse or sheltered warm courtyard in winter. As curry trees are relatively slow growing in temperate regions, they will last in a pot for many years. Trees are frost-tender but will often reshoot after even a heavy frost. These trees do best in full sun in moist, fertile soil with lots of humus. The soil must be well drained but make sure plants are watered often during dry weather.

Use Curry leaves have a strong almost rank flavour when fresh, but a delicious roasted curry flavour when cooked. They combine particularly well with vegetables, where they can be fried first until turning brown, and then the other ingredients added. In India, curry leaves are fried in combination with other spices and used in a wide range of curries giving a delicious flavour and aroma. Leaves are also added to traditional Indian chutneys. Because of the influence of Indian cuisine, curry leaves are now also used in fish curries prepared in Singapore and Malaysia. Markets in these countries sell special spice mixtures for fish which usually contain a few curry leaves. Frying the leaf maximises the flavour. Try frying a mixture of brown mustard seeds, curry leaves and crushed dried red chilli. Add this at the last minute to vegetable and lentil dishes. Use leaves to flavour basmati rice, or chop the leaves finely and add to yogurt to accompany curries. To maintain a supply over winter, freeze fresh leaves in a plastic bag and remove as needed. Leaves can also be dried but do not retain the true curry leaf flavour. The root and bark are both used medicinally.

Nasturtium officinale Brassicaceae

watercress

sai-yong choi (ChC); sai-eng chai (ChH); xi yang cai (ChM); selada-ayer (In); uotauresu (Ja); selada-ayer (Ma); lampaka (Ph); phakkat-nam (Th); xa lach xoong (Vi)

Watercress comes originally from Europe and the United Kingdom. The Ancient Romans recommended watercress and vinegar for anyone who was suffering from mental derangement, and ate it fresh to prevent hair loss. It was only introduced to Asia in the 19th century, but is now widely cultivated in western Asia.

Description A much-branched, aquatic, perennial plant, watercress has a low, creeping growth habit, with heart-shaped, bright green leaflets and white flowers. Roots grow from nodes where they touch the ground.

Cultivation Ideally watercress should be grown in running water, but it survives well in a pond with soil in the bottom that is topped up regularly with water; or in a pot that is always wet and semi-shaded. It should be grown from seed sown in spring, or from rooted pieces, and likes humus-rich, fertile soil and full sun. A piece of watercress left standing in a glass of water will grow roots in a couple of weeks. This piece can then be planted. Once plants are established remove any flower heads to promote leaf growth and prolong harvest.

Use Young shoots and leaves are eaten in salads and used as a garnish. In Asia, watercress is usually cooked before use and is often added to soups, although the Vietnamese eat it fresh with other salad greens, and add it fresh to soups just before serving. The Chinese make a special soup out of duck and watercress; they also fry watercress with fish or pork. In Japan this green herb is dipped into *tempura* batter and deep-fried. Watercress is high in vitamins A, B1, B2, C and E as well as calcium, copper, iron and magnesium. Medicinally, watercress is used as a laxative by the Chinese as well as a treatment for high blood pressure.

Nelumbo nucifera Nelumbonaceae

lotus root, loyus, sacred lotus, Indian lotus

lin ngau (rhizome), lin tze (seed) (ChC); lian (ChM); hasunone (Ja); akar teratai (Ma); hot sen kho (seed) (Vi)

Grown in China since the 12th century BC, lotus is associated with the goddess of Mercy, Kuan Yin, and Buddha. It is a sacred symbol of eternal life. This might have something to do with the longevity of its seeds, as seeds found in Chinese tombs over 5000 years old have been successfully germinated. Lotus are indigenous to northern Australia, Japan, China and parts of Iran and Russia, and are now cultivated all over the world. Small areas of commercial production can be seen in New South Wales, Northern Territory and Queensland.

(photograph courtesy Digger's Seeds)

Description This fast-spreading water plant grows from jointed tuberous roots with large, flat, circular leaves with wavy margins. The leaves can be as much as 80 cm across with stems as long as 2 m. Large scented pink or white flowers grow on long stalks up to 1 m above water level. Flowers appear in summer and are followed by flat-topped seed pods. There are many different cultivars, with flower colours ranging from white through pink to red. The tubers, when cut, display the characteristic air passages that make a slice of lotus resemble a flower.

Cultivation Lotus roots grow in still water. They are a summer crop that is planted in spring, grows through summer and dies back in winter. They need daytime maximums of 20° – 30°C for good growth and plenty of sunlight. Temperate climates produce higher quality rhizomes than tropical climates, and rhizomes will tolerate frosts because they are protected by water and mud. Lotus is most easily grown in a large pot in a mixture of one part loam and two to three parts old cow manure. They are not fussy about the pH of the soil. Place the pot in water so that it is just covered, and leave for two weeks. Now plant one rhizome, made up of several segments, in each pot. One end needs to be about 10 cm into the mud, while the other end just protrudes above the water. Start with water about 5 cm

(photograph by H.F. Chin)

deep and increase the depth (or move the pot into deeper water) as the rhizome grows. In warm tropical regions the final water depth can be as much as 3 metres, while in cooler temperate regions water depth can be as little as 30 cm, because the shallower the water the more quickly it will warm up. It is possible to grow lotus in very big jars or terracotta pots. They need to be about 500 L in size. In good conditions lotus plants can grow as much as 9 metres in one year. Initially only the leaves grow, with new rhizomes developing later in the season. Harvest mature rhizomes in autumn, after about four months' growth in warm climates, or when the leaves die off in cooler climates. Store, where there are no frosts, in tubs of moist sand. Harvest seed heads when the seed turns brown. Rhizomes can be left in the ground and harvested all year round where plants are abundant, and there is no chance of the rhizomes freezing. After harvesting rhizomes, reserve about 20% of the crop for replanting.

Plants can also be grown from seed which stays viable for many years. Earthcare Enterprises recommends carefully filing 1–2 mm off each end of the seed so that a hole is made in the dark seed coat but the seed flesh is not damaged. Soak seed in warm water on a sunny window sill, changing the water at least once a day. The seed should start to germinate after about three weeks, when they can either be left in the glass to watch them grow, or transferred to individual pots and just covered by water. Plants do not like to have their roots disturbed, so transplant to the final position after about two months and don't move again. When purchasing seed, make sure that they are from a variety that produces rhizomes, as there are some varieties that don't.

Use The rhizomes, young leaves, flower stalks and seeds are all eaten. Young rhizomes taste a little like artichokes and are added to stir-fries, salads and soups, as well as being deep-fried or cooked with other vegetables. They are also pickled in vinegar or syrup. Young leaves are eaten both raw and cooked, and used to wrap parcels of food, especially in China, where the parcels are then steamed. In Thailand, the leaf stems are eaten too. Seeds are roasted and eaten, or used in cooking like nuts. Prepare these seeds by first removing the seed coat and then cutting off the green plumule that is very bitter. Leaves and seeds can be dried for later use. Flower petals are used as a garnish and sprinkled over soup, while whole flowers are important in religious ceremonies, and all parts are used as medicine for a range of ailments. The leaves are used to treat diarrhoea and fevers, the seeds for diarrhoea and as a sedative, the flower pods are said to stop bleeding and the stamens to improve kidney function.

Ocimum spp.   Lamiaceae

O. basilicum Thai basil, anise basil, Asian sweet basil, liquorice basil

yu heung (ChC); yu xiang (ChM); chi neangvong (Kh); phak i tou (La); daun selaseh (Ma); horapha (Th); rau que (Vi)

O. americanum lemon basil, kemangi, hoary basil, hairy basil

daun kemangi (In); hom hor (La); daun kemangi (Ma); maenglak, bai manglak (Th)

O. tenuiflorum sacred basil, holy basil

surawung (In); i tou thai (La); kaphrao, krapow (Th)

Several different basils are commonly grown and used in Asian countries. Probably the most commonly seen are those known as Asian or Thai basil, lemon basil and sacred basil. Sacred or holy basil is sacred to Hindus. Sweet basil can be used as a substitute on most occasions. In Malaysia and Indonesia, the names of some varieties are interchangeable.

Description Most basils are annuals, and all should be treated as such in cool temperate climates. In tropical and subtropical regions, some basils, including sacred basil and lemon basil, are short-lived perennials. Sweet basil grows to about 50 cm with oval-shaped leaves and green bracts with white flowers that grow in tapering spikes at the top of the plant. The whole plant has a warm, clove-like scent and flavour. Sacred basil is smaller growing, has soft, hairy leaves and pink flowers. Thai basil has dark green, very aromatic leaves and purple flower heads, while lemon basil has leaves with a distinct lemon scent and that are softly hairy and smaller and paler green than sweet basil.

Thai basil

Cultivation Basil is a native of tropical areas, so needs plenty of warmth and moisture. Propagate from seed, sown either inside or in a greenhouse, and the seedlings transplanted outside after the last chance of frost is over. Space plants about 40 cm apart. In colder regions, protect young plants in the first weeks with a plastic guard — the easiest method is to cut the top and bottom from a plastic drink bottle and place this over the plant. When flowers appear, nip them back to encourage leaf growth. In warmer climates, basil is easily grown from cuttings taken in spring or summer. Basil grows best in rich fertile soils that are well drained. It needs full sun.

Use Basil leaves are often eaten raw in Thailand and Vietnam. For example basil is eaten with raw vegetables and a spicy dip or served with other fresh herbs and salad vegetables as a side dish. Add a handful of leaves, just before serving, to stir-fried meats like chicken or beef. The Malays use fresh basil leaves as a vegetable. Lemon basil can be fried with seafood while the seeds, soaked in water, are used in drinks or are added to coconut milk to make a dessert. Sacred basil has a sweet, spicy, pungent flavour and is used in salads, as a potherb and added to stir-fries and curries. Basils are also made into a fragrant tea and the oil from the leaves is used to treat coughs.

Oenanthe javanica Apiaceae

water celery, water drop wort, water parsley

sui kun (ChC); shui qin (ChM); pampung (In); seri (Ja); shelum (Ma); pak chi lawm (Th); can nuoc (Vi)

This water plant is a native of India, Japan, Malaysia and northern Australia. For hundreds of years it has been gathered from the wild and used as a food.

Description Water celery grows from branching, erect, angled stems with ovate, pinnate leaves with irregular indentations on the edges. The tiny white flowers grow in umbels at the top of the plant. The whole plant has a strong celery flavour.

Cultivation Water celery grows easily from seed or cuttings, with small pieces growing roots if left standing in a glass of water. Water celery can be grown in any container that holds water. It likes a good, composted soil enriched with manure. Cover with about 10 cm of water and leave to stand for a few days. Plant the water celery firmly into the soil and place in a sunny or semishaded position. Top up with fresh water at least once a week. Harvest stems and leaves as soon as the plant is big enough. This plant spreads rapidly, so thin out once a year if the pot becomes too crowded. It will easily colonise marshy areas, so make sure it doesn't escape into the wild.

Use Stems and leaves are eaten fresh in salads and added at the last minute to soups and stir-fries; the flavour combines particularly well with beef. They can also be steamed briefly and served as a vegetable with soy sauce. Raw, finely chopped leaves can be stirred into rice to give it a delicious celery flavour. The long slender white roots can also be eaten.

Pachyrhizus erosus   Fabaceae

yam bean, jicama, Mexican turnip, potato bean

sha kot, fan ko, sar got (ChC); ban kuang (ChH); sha ge, di gua, liang shu, dou shu (ChM); bangkuang (In); kuzuimo (Ja); pek kouk (Kh); man phao (La); benkuang, sengkuang (Ma); sinkamas (Ph); man kaeo (Th); cu dau (Vi)

Yam bean comes originally from tropical central and southern America, and was brought to Asia by the Spanish. It is now naturalised and widely grown in many tropical regions of Asia. The generic name *Pachyrhizus* comes from the Greek and means 'thick root'.

Description A strong-growing annual vine that can reach more than 6 m in length, the yam bean plant has large, three-lobed leaves and blue or white flowers that form in the leaf axils. These are fol-lowed by seed pods that are usually about 10 cm long. Each plant grows a swollen root tuber at its base. These are light brown and can be as heavy as 20 kg, but are usually harvested at a tenth of this size.

Cultivation Yam beans are grown from seed sown in early spring. They like full sun and a light, sandy soil with plenty of nutrients. Tubers only start to form after flowering commences in midsummer when the days get shorter. Remove flowers and seed pods to encourage tuber

sprinkled with lemon or lime juice. Traditionally in China, yam bean tubers are cooked and used to fill spring rolls. They can also be boiled, baked and fried. The flesh is white and crisp without a strong flavour, so it is a useful substitute for bamboo shoots and water chestnuts. Young, tender seed pods are also eaten but as the pods develop, their rotenone content increases. Rotenone is a poison, used by some peoples to kill fish, and is a constituent of derris dust. So mature seed pods are poisonous and should not be eaten.

growth. Plants are frost-tender, so harvest tubers before frosts begin. Yam beans need a long, hot, humid summer to develop tubers of any size, and plants that are exposed to day lengths as long as 15 hours will not produce tubers. For these reasons, yam beans are really only a proposition in tropical and subtropical climates. Support plants on poles or a trellis and allow about 60 cm between plants.

Use The large roots can be eaten raw or cooked. They can be eaten at any size. If buying tubers look for ones that are not cracked or bruised. They will store for a long time in the refrigerator, but over time starch is converted into sugar, making them less palatable. Yam bean tubers are eaten fresh like a fruit, or chopped and added to fruit/vegetable salads, known as *rojak* in Malaysia. Chopped fresh tubers are served with a chilli sauce, or simply

Pandanus amaryllifolius   Pandanaceae

pandan, screwpine

ban lan ye (ChM); daun pandan (In); sloeuk toeuy (Kh); teui hom (La); pandan wangi, daun pandan (Ma); toei hom, bay toey hom (Th); la dua (Vi)

Pandan probably comes originally from India and is now widely cultivated in South-East Asia.

Description This plant grows as a shrubby clump of long, flat, blade-like leaves to about 1.5 m. The fragrant leaves are arranged in spirals and can be 80 cm long. Pandan seldom if ever flowers.

Cultivation Pandans are easily grown in damp, tropical regions. They like full sun or semishade and any reasonable, well-drained soil. Feed with seaweed fertiliser every few weeks during spring and summer. Allow the plants to dry out over winter, watering only occasionally. Grow new plants from cuttings. In cooler regions, grow plants in pots and keep wellwatered in dry summers. In summer, stand the pot in a saucer of gravel that is regularly topped up with water to keep humidity as high as possible. Where winters are cold and wet it is essential that plants are allowed to dry out; water only infrequently and never allow water on the leaves. Repot in late spring and early summer.

Use The distinctive earthy fragrance of pandan leaves is used to enhance cooked rice, giving it the scent of freshly harvested hay. Leaves are usually fried with other spices in a little oil before the rice is added. Pandan leaves are also crushed or pounded to extract the juice that is then added to sweet dishes like jellies, desserts and cakes to add fragrance and a natural green colour. Alternatively, they can also be boiled in water and the water is then used to colour and flavour sweet dishes. In China and Malaysia, leaves are used to wrap food like prawns and chicken, and to make small containers for food. Young leaves are also cooked and eaten as a vegetable.

Perilla frutescens Lamiaceae

perilla, beefsteak plant

gee so (ChC); zi su (ChM); shiso (Ja); kkaennip namul (Ko); phak meng kheng (La); rau tia to, tai to (Vi)

Perilla comes originally from northern India, China, Korea and Japan, and is widely cultivated in these and other Asian countries. It has been used for centuries in China, both in cooking and in medicine.

Description Perilla is a fast-growing annual plant that reaches about 80 cm. It forms a compact shrub with large, ovate leaves with serrated edges, and spikes of small white or mauve flowers in autumn. There is a variety with green leaves, and another, more widely available, with crinkled red-magenta leaves. The leaves have distinctly different flavours so don't plant red and green varieties side by side as they

will cross-pollinate. There also appears to be variation in the red forms, with some plants showing a bronze tinge, while some have variable green and red leaves. 'Atropurpurea' has deep red-purple leaves and *P. frutescens* var. *nankinensis* has leaves with a bronze tinge and crinkled margins.

Cultivation Grow perilla from seed sown in spring or autumn. Sow the seed where it is to grow about 1 cm deep. Thin to about 25 cm between plants. In mild climates perilla will self-sow. Perilla grows best in a sunny position with well-drained soil to which compost and well-rotted manure has been added. In regions with very hot, dry summers, grow in semi-shade, or where it is protected from the hot afternoon sun. Varieties with red-bronze leaves are very ornamental and look fantastic combined with flowers in a decorative flower bed. In the tropics sow seed in autumn.

Use Leaves, flowers and seeds are all used, with flavours that are reminiscent of lemon, mint, cloves and basil. The seeds make a spicy garnish or pickle; the young red and green leaves are added to *sushi*, dipped in batter for *tempura* and added to soups. Red leaves are salted and pickled, as well as being used as wrapping for bite-sized pieces of shellfish, parcooked vegetables or daikon radish. Red and green leaves are used to flavour vinegars that can then be added to salads and dressings. Vinegar made using red perilla develops a deep pink colour. Sprouted seeds are also used as a garnish. In Japan, these are known as *mejiso*. In Vietnam, the leaves are added to salads and soups, eaten fresh in spring rolls and used to wrap grilled meats. The seeds are also the source of an oil that is used in some parts of Asia for drying (in paints, varnishes and for waterproofing), for cooking and as a fuel. Medicinally, a strong infusion of the leaves is used to reduce a temperature.

Persicaria odorata Polygonaceae

Vietnamese mint, knotweed, laksa leaf, laksa plant, Vietnamese coriander

laksa-yip (ChC); liao (ChM); azabutade (Ja); sang hom (Kh); phak pai nam (La); daun laksa, daun kesum (Ma); phak phai (Th); rau ram (Vi)

Vietnamese mint is not a true mint. It is native of South-East Asia, where it can be found growing wild on river banks and in swampy areas.

Description This sprawling plant grows in a clump with many-jointed stems (typical of the Polygonaceae family) to a height of 80 cm. The leaves, which grow alternately up the stems, are lanceolate and bright green with attractive, reddish-brown markings on the margins, more distinct on either side of the central vein near the base of the leaf. These markings often disappear in winter and/or when the plant is grown in a shady position. The small, pink flowers appear in late summer in slender, nodding spikes. The whole plant has a strange pungent scent and hot flavour.

Cultivation Vietnamese mint is best propagated from cuttings which will root in soil or water, or by detaching the outside stems which have sent out new roots where they have touched the soil. Space plants about 40 cm apart. Vietnamese mint will not tolerate frosts, so in very cold regions grow as an annual or in a pot so that it can moved inside in winter. It can also be grown in a hanging basket. Vietnamese mint likes a fertile soil with plenty of water, and will grow well on the edge of a pond. It does best in shade or semishade. If conditions are ideal it can be invasive, but is easily removed.

Use The leaves have a hot, peppery taste and are one of the strongest herbs used in Asian cooking. The older the leaves, the hotter the flavour. Leaves are used sparingly in both cold and hot dishes, but are often added at the last minute in hot dishes. They are added to noodle dishes in Malaysia, and eaten raw with spicy dips in Thailand. The Vietnamese wrap leaves around spring rolls with other herbs and lettuce, it is an essential ingredient of Vietnamese chicken salad, and is often sprinkled over fried chicken and chicken soups. Stems give a stronger flavour, and should be removed before serving.

Phaseolus lunatus Fabaceae

lima bean, Tonga bean, Java bean, sieva bean, Madagascar bean, butter bean

sai min tau, loi tau (ChC)

This plant can be traced back to Peru nearly 6000 years ago from archaeological remains found near the town of Paracas. The name lima, actually comes from the town Lima, in Peru, where this bean was first seen by Europeans.

Description This annual bean is a vigorous climber, although there are dwarf varieties that grow as bushes. It has racemes of white and pink flowers that are followed by short, flat, curved pods. There are several varieties of different heights and with different seed colours. Ripe, coloured seeds contain poisonous substances that can be removed by boiling, whereas the white seeds have none, so these are more usually grown. Plants generally fall into one of two groups either large-seeded or small-seeded.

Cultivation Sow at any time of the year in the tropics, and from spring to early summer in regions with hot summers. This bean does not grow well in cooler climates. It likes full sun and a fertile, nutrient-rich, well-drained soil. Add well-rotted manure and compost before planting. Sow seed about 3 cm deep and expect them to germinate in about 10 days at soil temperatures of around 22°C. Climbing varieties need a trellis and should be spaced about 25 cm apart, while bush varieties need to be spaced about 60 cm apart. Harvesting can generally begin about six weeks later for bush varieties or 2–3 months for climbing varieties. Harvest fresh beans as soon as the seed is mature and has swollen in the pod, but before the pod has dried out. Dried beans are harvested when the pods have dried but before they split.

Use Both fresh and dried beans are eaten, but they are always removed from the pod first. Since coloured beans contain poisonous cyanogenetic glucosides, they need to be soaked and boiled to remove these poisons. Fresh beans are shelled, boiled and added to soups and stews. Dried beans are used in the same way but need to be soaked first. The Chinese

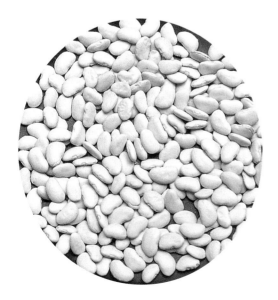

sprout the seeds and use them in vegetable dishes, while the Japanese use the cooked beans to make a sweetened paste known as *an*. In Indonesia and Malaysia, cooked beans are fermented to make *tempeh*.

Piper nigrum Piperaceae

pepper

lada, merica (In); mric (Kh); phrik thai (La); lada, lada hitam (Ma); phrik thai (Th); tieu (Vi)

This pepper vine came originally from the Malabar coast of India, but is now cultivated or found growing in most tropical regions. This is the pepper widely used in Western cooking.

Description Pepper is a perennial woody climber that can grow as much as 5 m in one season. The shiny, green, alternate leaves are elliptical with pointed tips, while flowers are borne in spikes that hang down, and are followed by small, rounded fruit that start off green and turn to red when ripe.

Cultivation Pepper vines grow most readily in humid tropical regions. They like a rich, well-drained soil and a shady position. In their natural habitat they happily grow up trees. When grown commercially, the vine is trained on a wooden pole so that it forms a tall column about 4 m high and 1.5 m in diameter. Pepper is most easily grown from cuttings taken in spring, but it can also be grown from seed. It does not do well in temperate regions unless it is grown in a heated greenhouse.

Use Peppercorns from *Piper nigrum* vines come in three forms, green, white and black. Green peppercorns are young berries that have either been pickled or freeze-dried while still fresh. These are sometimes added to Thai dishes to provide extra piquancy and flavour. White peppercorns are produced by harvesting ripe, red berries, removing the red skins and drying in the sun until the seed is white. Powdered white pepper is widely used in China. Black pepper is made from unripe (green) berries that are sun-dried until they turn black. Black pepper is an essential ingredient of most curry powders, and before chillies were introduced to Asia in the 1500s it was even more widely used.

Leaves and green berries

Piper sarmentosum   Piperaceae

wild pepper, pepper leaves, pointed pepper, betel leaves

kadok (In); chaplou (Kh); bai som phou (La); daun kaduk (Ma); chaa phluu, cha plu (Th); la lot (Vi)

This shade-loving pepper is indigenous to Thailand and Vietnam, and is a cultivated plant in other Asian countries such as Malaysia and Indonesia. Although sometimes called betel leaves, this plant should not be confused with the other betel pepper (*P. betle*), the leaves of which are chewed with betel nut (a fruit from a particular palm) and lime in many parts of South-East Asia and New Guinea.

Description Wild pepper grows to about 90 cm with hairy stems and shiny, green, ovate leaves. The small white flowers occur in spikes.

Cultivation This pepper does not climb in the same way as *P. nigrum*, but is otherwise grown in the same way.

Use The pungent, spicy leaves are either blanched and eaten as a vegetable, or eaten raw, especially in salads. The leaves are also used to wrap small pieces of food. Try soaking the leaves in cold water with a little added sugar for two hours before use. This not only helps to freshen them but also subtly alters the flavour. In Thailand, wild pepper is used to wrap raw ginger, peanuts, shrimps, shallots and lime to make delicious small snacks. In northern Malaysia, the leaves are finely sliced and added to rice salads. Wild pepper leaves are also widely used medicinally for complaints as diverse as asthma, toothache and headache.

Plectranthus amboinicus Lamiaceae

Cuban oregano, five-seasons herb, five-in-one herb, country borage, Indian borage, Spanish thyme, Mexican mint

pok hor (ChC); po ho (ChH); daun kucing, daun kambing (In); daun bangun-bangun (Ma); tan day la (Vi)

This herb probably came originally from India and tropical Africa, but can now be found growing wild in many tropical countries. It is also grown in gardens throughout tropical Africa, India, South-East Asia and central America and can often be seen for sale in local markets in these countries.

Description The whole plant is succulent and softly hairy. The sprawling pale green stems grow from a central root to a height of 70 cm. The thick, scalloped, opposite leaves grow on short stems and are pale green, sometimes with reddish markings. There is a variegated form where the leaves have pale yellow margins. The flowers are pale pink and grow in short terminal spikes. The whole plant has a strong scent similar to oregano, but with an extra spiciness.

Cultivation Propagate Cuban oregano from seed or cuttings taken in spring and grown under cover in the early stages. Cuban oregano is a perennial tropical plant that will not survive cold, damp weather. For this reason it grows easily in

Variegated Cuban oregano

the tropics, but is best regarded as an annual in really cold regions. It grows well in a pot and makes an interesting candidate for a hanging basket. In cooler regions, try moving it inside to a sunny windowsill in winter, make sure not to overwater, and it may be possible to keep it alive through winter. In tropical regions, grow Cuban oregano in a sunny position in well-drained soil — don't ever let it get too wet. From time to time, nip back new growth to encourage a bushier habit.

Use The flavour of the leaf is strong and resembles thyme and oregano, so use it sparingly. Cuban oregano, finely chopped, can be sprinkled into soups, stews, and egg and tomato dishes. In Malaysia and Indonesia, leaves are added to strongly flavoured fish and meat dishes, like goat and mutton. The flavour of the leaves combines particularly well with beans, so try stirring a finely chopped leaf into bean salad or soup. In India, leaves are dipped in batter and fried, as well as being used to treat coughs. The Vietnamese add this herb to sweet and sour soup, and use it to treat headaches, sore throats and fever. The leaves are also made into a pleasant tasting tea.

Psophocarpus tetragonolobus   Fabaceae

winged bean, four-angled bean, Goa bean, Manila bean, princess bean, asparagus pea, asparagus bean, climbing winged bean.

say lim tau (ChC); see kak atau (ChH); si jiao dou (ChM); kecipir (In); popiey (Kh); mak thoua phou (La); kachang belimbing, kakang botol (Ma); seguidilla, sigarilyas (Ph); thua phu (Th); dau rong (Vi)

It has been suggested that winged beans come originally from tropical Asia or from Madagascar or from India. Regardless of their source they are now widely grown from India to New Guinea.

Description Grown for their beans and tubers, winged beans are perennial trailing climbing plants with thick, fibrous roots. Only some varieties produce tubers. The leaves are dark green and trifoliate. Flowers are pink to mauve-blue, or sometimes white, and are followed by unusual four-angled green pods with wavy margins. Pods are up to 30 cm long and contain 5 – 20 round green seeds which turn brown or black when mature.

Cultivation Winged beans are tropical plants that can also be grown in the subtropics. They are very sensitive to day length and require short days of only 11 – 13 hours daylight before they will begin to flower. As they are also frost-sensitive, they are not suitable for many temperate regions.

They are not fussy about soil as long as it is well drained, but for good bean production need to be grown up a trellis in full sun. If they are being grown for tubers only, then the trellis is not necessary. Seed only stays viable for about one year. Plant in late spring to early summer in the tropics, and early spring inside in subtropical

regions. Move outside once the last chance of frost is over. Grow plants from seed, which needs to be treated to help germination. Either rub with sandpaper, or nick the surface with a knife or drop into water that has just boiled and leave until the water is cold. Plant seeds about 2 cm deep and 60 cm apart. Keep well watered during dry weather but never over water. Begin to harvest beans about 10 weeks after sowing, while tubers are harvested between four and eight months after sowing. Winged beans have a very high nitrogen-fixing ability so they are a useful rotation crop.

Use   Young shoots and leaves can be picked and cooked as a vegetable; they are probably best steamed. Flower buds and flowers have a flavour reminiscent of mushrooms and can be eaten raw or lightly stir-fried, while the root tubers can be baked, roasted and boiled. Young pods taste like asparagus and are the part most commonly eaten. They are harvested when about 10 cm long, at which point they are only half-grown, and can be eaten raw in salads, or cooked. Boil or steam them whole and serve them as a vegetable, or slice and drop into a stir-fry, or add to soup. The Thais blanch the beans in hot water, plunge into cold water, drain and then marinate in lime juice before serving as a salad. In Japan, flowers are dipped into *tempura* batter and deep-fried. The protein content of the tubers can be as high as 20% (in potatoes it is typically less than 7%).

(photograph by H.F. Chin)

116

Raphanus sativus   Longipinnatus Group
Brassicaceae

Chinese radish, Japanese radish, daikon

loh bak, loh pak (ChC); peh chai tau (ChH); luo bo, lai fu (ChM); lobak (In); daikon (Ja); they thav (Kh); hua phak kat (La); lobak putih (Ma); labano (Ph); phak khi hut (Th); cu cai trang (Vi)

The exact origin of this vegetable is unknown, as it has been cultivated by humans since before recorded history. Chinese radishes have been eaten in Asia since at least 400 BC. They are now grown throughout tropical Asia and also grown commercially in all mainland Australian states.

Description   This annual vegetable grows as a rosette with narrow, dark green, deeply incised leaves. From this rosette of leaves grows a long, cylindrical, oblong or spherical white root that can weigh as much as 5 kg. More unusually, roots can also be yellowish, green and black. There are many different varieties and cultivars available.

Cultivation   Chinese radishes are a cold climate crop that grows well in New South Wales and Victoria. Sowing times are spring and early autumn, depending on the variety. Ideal daytime maximum tempera-

'Minowase Summer'

tures for growth are between 20 – 25°C. Too much sunlight can cause pithiness and/or internal browning. Seed will germinate at soil temperatures as low as 5 °C, but if temperatures are too low when seed is sown (less than 10°C), then plants may bolt to seed before the roots get a chance to develop properly. Cooler temperatures are less important once plants are well developed. Sow seed direct into shallow drills 2 cm deep. Seed should germinate in about four to seven days at soil temperatures around 21°C. Chinese radishes like a deep, rich, light, well-drained and well-cultivated soil with a pH of 6.0 – 6.5. If soils are too heavy the roots will be bent and twisted. They grow best in raised beds to which manure and compost have been added a

few weeks before planting. Thin seedlings to about 25 cm between plants. Regular water is important because roots must grow rapidly if they are to be mild and tender. Time to maturity varies depending on the cultivar and time of year, but it can be anywhere from 50 to 90 days. Harvest when the diameter of the neck is 5 cm or more. Plant edible chrysanthemum in rotation with Chinese radish to help reduce pests and diseases.

Use Chinese radishes are usually cooked as a vegetable, but they can be eaten raw, especially in salads. Try slicing them and stir-frying or add chunks to soup or stews. The Japanese grate radish and add it to soy sauce to make a dipping sauce for *tempura*. Radishes are also dried, pickled, fermented and soaked in brine. In Korea, these radishes are used to make *kimchi*. The pungent flavour of radishes is found mainly in the skin, so to reduce heat, peel the skin off before eating or cooking. The leaves are also eaten as a vegetable, steamed or stir-fried, and young flower heads can be treated in the same way. The whole plant is rich in carotene and calcium, while the roots contain vitamin C, potassium and dietary fibre as well. Chinese cooks prefer pure white, long narrow forms of Chinese radish, while the Japanese prefer thicker roots with green necks, which usually have a milder flavour.

Sagittaria sagittifolia Alismataceae

arrowhead, Chinese potato, swamp potato

chi gu (ChM); kuwai (Ja)

This water plant is probably native to Japan and China, where it is also widely cultivated. It is now naturalised in ponds and slow moving waterways in many parts of Europe, Asia and America.

Description Arrowhead is a perennial plant that grows to about 70 cm from spherical, brownish-yellow corms. The leaves that grow on long slender stems are pale green and shaped like arrowheads. They can be up to 20 cm wide and 30 cm long. The three-petalled flowers are white with a yellow centre.

Cultivation Arrowhead can be planted on the edge of a pond, or grown in a bath tub or similar container. It is a plant that does best in temperate regions but will survive in a subtropical climate. Arrowhead grows best with 100 – 300 mm of water over the soil; the colder the climate the more shallow the water should be. Plant the corms in spring by pushing down into mud that has been enriched with cow manure. Choose a sunny position and space the corms about 30 cm apart. In autumn, horizontal rhizomes grow from the central corm and a new corm will grow at the end of each rhizome. Harvest corms in autumn. In China, the corms are sometimes dropped into small vessels containing water and

allowed to sprout, so that the leaves can be harvested.

Use Young shoots, leaves and corms can all be eaten. Young shoots and leaves can be eaten raw or cooked but corms are always cooked. They are peeled and sliced, then fried or added to stews. They have a slightly sweet taste. Corms can also be boiled, roasted or baked. In China, the corms are chopped and cooked with meats like pork in stir-fries, or chopped and fried to make chips.

Sauropus androgynus Euphorbiaceae

sauropus, sweet leaf, katuk

ma ni chai (In); cekur manis (Ma); phak waan baan (Th)

Sauropus is found growing wild in Malaysia and India. It is also cultivated in both these and other Asian countries.

Description This shrub or small tree grows to about 3 m. It has slender, grey-green branches with alternate, oval to lance-shaped leaves. The delicate flowers are yellow or yellow and red and the fruit is pink and rounded. Inside the fruit are black seeds. Both the flowers and fruit hang down underneath the leaves.

Cultivation Grow from stem cuttings or by sowing fresh seed. Sauropus will grow in most soils and tolerates sun and semi-shade. Fertilise regularly to encourage leafy growth. Begin to harvest leaves and shoots after about two months, and prune hard once it starts to get tall because plants are prone to falling over. Sauropus is frost-tender but will often reshoot from ground level after a heavy frost.

Use Leaves and young shoots have a delicate, peanut flavour and are used in stir-fries and soup, while the fruits are cooked and added to desserts or used to colour jam. It is an important vegetable in Borneo where it is eaten cooked and raw. In Malaysia, it is eaten as a vegetable, while in Indonesia, it is used to colour food. Sauropus leaves can also be added to salads. In Thailand, young leaves are blanched or fried and eaten as a vegetable, as well as being stirred into soup and added to fish curries. Traditionally, in Malaysia, a poultice is made out of roots and leaves to treat ulcers, and a decoction made from the roots to treat fever.

120

Sechium edule Cucurbitaceae

choko, chayote, vegetable pear, mirliton, mango squash

sun ren gua, li gua (ChM); labu siam (Ma)

Chokos come originally from central and southern America but they are now widely grown in tropical regions of Asia.

Description This perennial plant is a very vigorous climber capable of growing up to 12 m in one season. It has furrowed stems and pointed, lobed leaves. Flowers are a creamy-green with solitary female flowers and male flowers in groups, all on one plant. The pear-shaped fruit has bright green skin with white flesh and a single, flat seed inside, and is produced most prolifically during autumn and winter. There are also varieties with light green and white skins.

Cultivation Grow from seeds or stem cuttings or just plant the whole fruit. Plant in spring in most areas, and in autumn as well in the tropics, with the narrow end just protruding from the soil. Individual plants need to be about 3 m apart and much more fruit will be produced if plants can grow up a trellis or a tree. Don't overfertilise or there will be lots of leaves and no fruit. Add a little compost or manure at planting and when the fruit begin to swell. Harvest young fruit three to four months after planting. The whole plant is cold-sensitive so won't tolerate frost, and it doesn't like its roots too wet.

Use Seeds, young leaves and tendrils can be eaten, but it is the fruit that is mostly used. This is occasionally eaten raw but usually cooked as a vegetable, where it can be baked, stuffed, fried, boiled, mashed, buttered or pickled. The flavour is similar to zucchini. It is also stir-fried with meat or seafood and can be added to soup. Seeds have a delightful nutty flavour and can be fried and eaten. If buying fruit, make sure it is firm with no bruises, and that it hasn't started to germinate; if the seeds inside have germinated there will be young seedlings growing from the broad end of the fruit. Always place chokos into plastic bags for storage as this helps to maintain humidity and stop the choko from shrivelling. They do not like to be stored at air temperatures below 10°C.

Sesbania grandiflora Fabaceae

sesban, scarlet wisteria vine, vegetable hummingbird, agati

kakang turi (Ma), khae baan, khae daeng (Th)

The plant is indigenous to northern and eastern Asia and is grown throughout India and South-East Asia.

Description Sesban is a fast-growing, perennial tree that is usually short-lived. It grows to about 6 m and has alternate, pinnate leaves with numerous leaflets. The large, showy, white flowers occur in summer and are followed by long, narrow green pods that can be 30 cm long and contain as many as 50 seeds.

Cultivation Grow from seeds sown in spring; they germinate best at soil temperatures of about 19 °C. Sesban can also be grown from cuttings. This plant is frost-tender, needs full sun, plenty of water during dry weather and reasonably fertile, well-drained soil. Don't overwater in cold weather. In temperate regions, this tree can be grown in a pot and moved into a sheltered warm position or into a greenhouse in winter.

Use The white flowers have a mushroomy taste and can be eaten raw or blanched. They are also added to curries, soups and stews. Flowers are high in sugar and iron. Young pods are also eaten, usually cooked as a vegetable and young leaves and shoots can be cooked and eaten too.

Solanum sp.   Solanaceae

S. *melongena* eggplant, brinjal, aubergine

ai kua (ChC); qie zi (ChM); terung (In); nasu (Ja); trap (Kh); mak kheua (La); terung, terong (Ma); makhua, makua (Th); ca (Vi)

S. *torvum* pea eggplant

shu qie zi (ChM); terong pipit (Ma)

Eggplants probably come originally from India, where wild plants are still seen today, although the earliest record of their use is from China. The species name, *melongena*, comes from Arabic. The pea eggplant is widely grown in the tropical Asia, but is probably most common on the Malay peninsula.

Description Eggplants grown for Asian cuisine come in a variety of shapes (golf ball, apple, egg, cigar), sizes and colours (red, white, purple, yellow, green and combinations of these), but the most common are probably long, slender and purple. All eggplants are short-lived perennials that are usually grown as annuals. They grow as branched shrubs to 1.5 m with a woody base and hairy stems. The simple, green leaves are softly hairy, and the flowers, which come in a range of purples, occur either singly or in clusters. Pea eggplant grows as a bush to about 2 m with spiny stems and round, slightly lobed leaves. Mauve flowers are followed by pea-sized fruit which turn yellow when ripe.

Cultivation Eggplants are grown from seed sown in spring in tropical and tem-

S. melogena

perate regions. Plant out seedlings about 50 cm apart, after the last chance of frost is over, into well-prepared, nutrient-rich soil in full sun. Water regularly because

123

drought stress causes bitterness. Start harvesting fruit about three months later. Fruit should be shiny and firm with a good strong colour. Dull skin or brown colours usually indicate that the fruit is overmature and so will be hard and bitter.

Use Use fruit as soon as possible after harvest. Eggplants are used, usually sliced, in stir-fries. They can also be roasted whole, sliced or stuffed, or added to casseroles and stews. The long, white variety seems to be most popular in China, while Malaysians and Indonesians prefer

S. torvum

the long purple type, and Indians the egg-shaped purple variety. The green, unripe fruit of pea eggplant is added to curries in Malaysia and the root is used medicinally.

Stachys affinis Lamiaceae

Chinese artichoke, Japanese artichoke, crosnes, spirals

kon loh (ChC); gan lu, cao shi can (ChM); choro-gi (Ja)

Chinese artichokes are not related to either the globe or the Jerusalem artichoke. They have been grown in China and other parts of Asia for centuries, but were first seen in Europe in the 1880s, when they were sent to France by the physician to the Russian Embassy in China. They were planted at Crosnes in France and so became known in Europe as crosnes. Chinese artichokes probably first came to Australia with Chinese miners during the gold rushes in the 19th century, but have only recently become more widely available.

Description Chinese artichokes grow as sprawling, herbaceous plants to about

70 cm with oval, grey-green leaves and mauve flowers that occur in spikes. The corkscrew-shaped tubers grow at the end of the roots and look a bit like witchetty grubs. When first harvested, they have an attractive, translucent sheen but this fades after a couple of days.

Cultivation Plant seed or tubers in spring in any reasonable soil that has not been recently fertilised. Too much fertiliser will cause abundant leaf growth but few tubers. Tubers should be planted about 5 cm deep and 30 cm apart. They do best in a temperate climate in full sun with well-drained soil. Water well during dry weather. The whole plant dies back in late autumn, and this is when the tubers are ready to harvest. Harvest the tubers as they are needed, but if they have to be harvested all at once, they will keep in the refrigerator in water with a little lemon juice for about a month. Plant Chinese artichokes in a bed of their own or in a spot where they can be contained as they can be invasive.

Use After harvesting, prepare the tubers by washing and scrubbing gently until the dirt is removed. They don't need to be peeled. Chinese artichoke tubers have a mild, nutty flavour but are used more for their crunchy texture rather than their flavour. They are used raw with dips or in salads, or can be cooked in stir-fries, soups and stews. Tubers can also be boiled or steamed and served as they are or with a sauce. Generally five to eight minutes cooking time is sufficient.

Tamarindus indica Fabaceae

tamarind

asam jawa (In); ampil (Kh); mak khame (La); asam jawa (Ma); sampalok (Ph); ma khaam (Th); me (Vi)

This attractive tree comes originally from Africa but is now found in many other countries, where it is grown as a shade tree as well as for its fruit.

Description Tamarind is a tall (to 30 m), elegant, tropical tree with fine leaves and fragrant, cream or yellow flowers with red stripes. The bean-like fruit have brittle

(photograph courtesy Digger's Seeds)

brown shells and contain large, hard seeds surrounded by a tangy pulp.

Cultivation Tamarind trees will grow in dry regions as well as areas that get regular water, but they are essentially tropical plants. Although frost-tender when young, they will tolerate several degrees of frost once well established. They are not fussy about soil as long as it is well drained. They like full sun and will tolerate wind and salt spay. Tamarind trees are sometimes grown by bonsai enthusiasts. In temperate regions grow tamarind in a large pot and move to a warm, sheltered, sunny position in winter. These trees produce pods when quite small, so pot-grown specimens will often produce pods. In some countries, tamarind is planted very close together, and young seedlings harvested as a vegetable when they are only 30 cm high.

Use Fresh sprigs of young leaves and flowers of the tamarind tree are eaten as a vegetable in Thailand. In the Philippines, the sprigs are added to soups to lend a sour taste to the accompanying food. Leaves and flowers can also be stirred into salads, and young green pods can be used in the same ways. The pulp of ripe fruit is eaten fresh and in dips, or it is sometimes coated in sugar and made into a sweet. Most commonly, the tangy pulp is used to make a refreshing drink or to add a pleasant, acid, sour taste to wide range of dishes. The pulp is rich in B complex vitamins and minerals. Seeds can also be roasted and eaten.

Tamarind pods with one broken to show the pulp

126

Trichosanthes cucumerina var. *anguina*
Cucurbitaceae

snake gourd

pe-lin-nwe (Bu); sair kua (ChC); mang gua, she gua (ChM); ketola ular (Ma); buap nguu (Th)

The generic name, *Trichosanthes*, comes from a Greek word meaning 'hair flower' and refers to the white, delicately fringed flower. Snake gourds come originally from India. They are now grown in most tropical regions of the world and grown commercially in Australia in New South Wales, Northern Territory and Queensland.

Description This annual climbing plant has angular stems and softly hairy, lobed leaves. The male and female flowers occur on the same plant and are white, fringed and sweetly scented. Fruit are long, narrow and twisted, some reaching 120 cm in length.

Cultivation Snake gourds grow well in humid, tropical regions. In Darwin, they are grown from late March to June. They grow best at daytime maximums of 30° – 35°C, and don't do well at temperatures below 20°C. Grow from seed planted directly into a raised bed with 60 cm between plants. Train up a tripod, or trellis of about 2 m in height, if possible using a trellis that forms a 'roof'. Snake gourds like full sun and a relatively rich but well-drained soil, because they don't like to be waterlogged. They also need plenty of moisture during growth, so water regularly without flooding. Start harvesting fruit when they are over 30 cm long but still green and tender — this usually takes about three weeks from fruit set. Snake gourds grow naturally with a twisted shape (hence the name). A small weight attached to the base, while the gourd is young, will result in straight fruit.

Snake gourd vine and fruit at Shipards Herb Farm

127

Use Immature fruits can be sliced and fried, or boiled as a vegetable. They are also added to curries, cut in half, stuffed and baked, or stir-fried with other vegetables. More mature fruits are added to soup. Fully mature fruits are bitter and tough because of the fibres, but are highly regarded for their medicinal value. Shoots and young leaves are also cooked as vegetable and eaten.

Trigonella foenum-graecum Fabaceae

fenugreek

halba (Ma)

Fenugreek has been used as a fodder plant for centuries — hence its name, *foenum-graecum*, meaning 'Greek hay'.

Description Fenugreek is a slender, low-growing herb with alternate leaves made up of three leaflets, oblong in shape and soft green in colour. Flowers are yellowish-white and grow in the axils of the upper leaves. These are followed by long, sickle-shaped pods containing 10-20 yellow-brown seeds.

Cultivation Fenugreek is grown from seed sown in spring and autumn. Sow into humus-rich soil in full sun. This seed germinates easily. Thin to about 20 cm between plants. Leaves are ready to harvest after about four weeks, and seeds after eight to ten weeks. Because they are fast-growing, successive sowings are

needed to ensure a regular supply. Fenugreek will tolerate cold and frost, but does not like to be too dry, so keep plants well watered during dry periods. Harvest leaves while the plants are still young and before flowers appear, otherwise the stems and leaves will be tough. For a quick salad plant, sow in pots or boxes and harvest very young, when only a few leaves have grown.

Use Very young plants are added to salads, and the seed can be sprouted for salads and stir-fries. Older leaves are chopped and lightly fried with other herbs, leafy vegetables and spices and served as a vegetable dish. The lightly roasted seeds are an ingredient in curries, pickles and chutneys. The flavour is strong and pungent, so never use too many at once. Both the seeds and leaves of fenugreek are used medicinally and in veterinary science. Tea made from the seeds reduces fever, eases digestive and menstrual pain and acts as a general tonic. Leaves or seed fed to animals has the same effect and also increases the milk supply from feeding mothers. The whole plant is high in protein and vitamins including vitamin E, and it also contains calcium and phosphorus.

Vigna angularis Fabaceae

adzuki bean, Chinese red bean, andanka beans

hong xiao dou, chi dou (ChM); azuki (Ja); dau do (Vi)

This bean comes originally from China and Japan, where it is still cultivated today. In Japan, it is the second most important dry bean crop grown.

Description Adzuki beans grow as a bush to about 60 cm with leaves resembling those of peas. Yellow flowers are followed by groups of smooth cylindrical pods. These pods contain shiny oval seeds that are smaller than ordinary bean seeds, and usually dark red with a protruding ridge on one side.

Cultivation Grow adzuki beans by planting seeds in spring directly into fertile, well-drained soil with a pH of 5.5 – 6.5. They like full sun. In tropical regions, plant in autumn. Place seeds about 20 cm apart in rows about 60 cm apart. Water regularly and top-dress with manure after about one month's growth. Begin to harvest young green beans when the seed starts to swell inside the pod. Keep picking every five days or so. Beans take up to four months to reach maturity. Pick mature pods once they are fully ripe but before they dry, when they will shatter and drop the seeds to the ground. Harvest by pulling the whole plant from the ground and stacking in a dry, airy position for a couple of weeks; then remove the beans from the pod and store in a sealed, airtight jar in the refrigerator.

Use Dried beans are soaked for two hours before cooking for another two hours. They can then be added to soups and stews. Dried beans are also ground into a bean meal and made into a sweet paste which is often used in desserts. Beans are also sprouted to produce sprouts with a delicious nutty flavour. The whole immature pod is cooked and eaten like French beans. Adzuki beans are used to make *hoisin sauce*.

Vigna radiata   Fabaceae

mung bean

kakang djong, kacang eedjo (In); yaenari (Ja); akang hijau (Ma); munggo (Ph); tau ngok (Th); dau xanh (Vi)

Mung beans are a native of India, where they have been cultivated for centuries as a food crop. They are now grown all over tropical Asia.

Description Mung bean plants are erect, sprawling annuals that grow to about 40 cm, with hairy, trifoliate leaves and hairy stems. Pale yellow flowers are followed by long, narrow, cylindrical, green pods that turn grey or brown. Each pod contains between 8 – 15 green, gold or black seeds.

Cultivation Grow from seed in the same way as adzuki beans (see page 00). Plants will tolerate quite dry conditions but are frost-sensitive. Harvest young pods after about two months, and mature pods (for the ripe seeds) one to two months later. Harvest dried beans as for adzuki beans.

Use Both young pods and young leaves can be eaten raw or cooked, but this plant is better known for its seeds. These are used for sprouting and to produce bean flour. Seeds and bean flour are cooked and used in soups and stews. Fresh seeds are also added to soups and stews, while sprouted seed is eaten raw or stir-fried. Thin translucent noodles, commonly used in Vietnam and China, are often made from mung bean flour. Straw from the harvested plants is used as fodder, and the golden-seeded variety is often grown specifically for fodder.

(photograph by H.F. Chin)

131

Vigna unguiculata ssp. *sesquipedalis*   Cucurbitaceae

snakebean, asparagus bean, yard-long bean, Chinese long bean

cheung kong tau, dau kok, dau gok (ChC); chang dou, cai dou, jiang dou, chang jiang dou (ChM); kacang tunggak, kacang panjang (In); sasage (Ja); sandaek ku (Kh); mak thoua niao (La); kacang panjang (Ma); sitao, banor (Ph); thua fak yao (Th); dau dua, dau que (Vi)

Snakebeans are widely grown throughout tropical Asia, and are grown commercially in New South Wales, Northern Territory, Queensland and Victoria.

Description There are dwarf and climbing types. Climbing forms will take longer to produce beans, but then produce for longer. Twining stems can be as long as 4 m, and leaves are trifoliate. Yellow or mauve flowers grow on long stems and are followed by fleshy bean pods that occur in pairs and can be green, white or a reddish-purple. Beans can be as long as 50 cm but they are at their tastiest at about 25 cm. They are stringless.

Cultivation Ideally, these beans grow in climates with warm summers where daytime maximums are 25° – 35°C, and night-time temperatures do not drop below 15°C. They will grow in cooler regions but will not produce as well. Most cultivars are affected by day length and will not flower until after the days start to get shorter in summer. Snakebean will grow in most soils as long as the pH is 5.5 – 7.5. Plant seeds about 2 cm into damp soil in raised beds or ridges, 40 cm between plants for climbing forms, and 25 cm for dwarf forms. Seeds can take up to 12 days to germinate, even at optimum soil temperatures (around 20°C). In cooler climates, plant in late spring and early summer, while in the tropics, plant from early spring to late summer. Water only after four days, when germination should have begun. This helps to stop seed from rotting. Climbing forms need trellises of about 2 m; as the young plants grow, train them up the vertical supports. Water regularly during dry weather. Flowering should start about five weeks after the seeds are sown, and beans will be ready to harvest about three weeks after that. Pick beans before or when they reach their full length (over 30 cm), but before the seeds begin to swell. Don't leave beans on the plant to harden and produce seed, unless they are to be collected and sown the following year, because this exhausts the plant.

Use Snakebeans taste similar to green beans, but the texture is more dense. They do not need to be strung. Trim the ends off each bean before cutting to the desired length. The pods can be boiled, added to stir-fries or eaten raw. In China, the beans are cut into 3 cm lengths and stir-fried with egg. Reddish-purple snakebeans, unlike other beans of this colour, actually retain their colour when cooked. Leaves and young stems can also be steamed and eaten as a vegetable.

Vigna umbellata Fabaceae

rice bean, climbing-mountain bean, mambi bean, Oriental bean

mai tau (ChC); katjang otji (In); kachang sepalit (Ma); nho nhe (Vi)

Rice bean is a native of southern China and tropical South-East Asia, but it is widely cultivated throughout Asia.

Description Rice beans are fast-growing, vigorous, climbing beans with typical bean leaves. Flowers are a pale creamy-yellow and the ripe beans are green, turning brown at maturity. Each pod contains six to eight dark brown seeds.

Cultivation In the uplands of Vietnam, rice bean is often intercropped with corn. The corn matures first in the dry season and the rice bean then uses the dried stalks for support. The dense mass of bean

the rice beans are harvested, about eight months after planting, the residues of both crops are left on the soil surface as green manure. Often, fallen rice bean seeds self-sow, so that it is not necessary to replant the crop from year to year.

Grow rice beans in the same way as the climbing form of snakebean (see page 132).

Use Young leaves and beans are steamed whole and served as a vegetable with rice. They are also added to soups and stir-fries, and the seed can be sprouted and eaten. Rice beans are used in tropical regions as a cover crop to improve soils and as a fodder crop.

foliage protects the soil from heavy rains in the rainy season, while the plants add nitrogen for the use of future crops. When

Xanthosoma sp. *X. sagittifolium* and *X. brasiliense* Araceae

cocoyam, yautia, tannier, kang kong taro, malanga

woo-tau (ChC); yu tou (ChM); ubi keladi (Ma)

These plants come originally from tropical America but are now widely grown in the West Indies and Asia.

Description Cocoyams grow from a central corm with long stems and large leaves reminiscent of elephant ears. If cut, they exude a thick milky juice. Large yellow or white flowers grow in summer from the centre of the plant. As the plant grows the central corm produces numerous potato-sized tubers around it. The whole plant can be as tall as 1.5 m.

Cultivation Grow new plants by planting pieces of the central corm or whole tubers in spring. Place these 10 cm below the soil surface and about 80 cm apart. Although cocoyams like a nutrient-rich, damp soil they do not need as much moisture as taro, to which they are related. In very hot climates, grow these plants under shady trees; this will also help to protect them from frosts which may kill them. Plants can take more than a year to yield a reasonable crop. Cocoyams can be grown in temperate regions but need to be protected from frosts and will probably not produce any worthwhile tubers.

Use Cocoyams are grown for their carbohydrate-rich tubers, which also contain a moderate amount of protein and some vitamins and minerals. The starch in the tubers is very easily digested, and in Cuba, babies and people with ulcers are put on a diet of cocoyams. Never eat the tubers or leaves raw as they contain an acrid principle that can cause irritation, but is destroyed by heat. Wash and peel the tubers before cooking, although sometimes it may be necessary to cook first and then peel because some tubers are very

hard. Like potatoes, the tubers can be boiled, mashed, baked or roasted. Young leaves and stems are also eaten but these need to be well cooked before use. Add them to soups or stews or serve them as a vegetable similar to spinach.

Zingiber officinale   Zingiberaceae

ginger, green ginger

keong (ChC); kiew (ChH); jiang (ChM); jahe (In); shooga (Ja); khgney (Kh); saenggang, saeng (Ko); khing (La); halia (Ma); luya (Ph); khing (Th); gung (Vi)

The first written records of ginger come from Confucius (551–479 BC). Ginger moved from China to the Mediterranean with Arab traders, and Greek and Roman scholars mention it in the 1st century AD. The Spaniards took it to the West Indies, where some of the highest quality ginger is grown today. In medieval times, ginger

was widely used to disguise the flavour of rancid meat.

Description Ginger is a tropical perennial plant that grows to about 60 cm from a swollen, knobbly underground stem or rhizome with numerous buds. When conditions are right, each bud begins to grow,

producing upright pseudo-stems which can reach 1 m high, with long narrow dark green leaves branching out like a ladder on either side. Commercially grown ginger is usually sterile, but the wild forms sometimes produces a cluster of yellow or white flowers spotted with purple.

Cultivation Ginger does best in sandy, well-drained soil with plenty of organic matter. It can be grown from any small piece of rhizome that has a bud and is planted in early spring. Plant just below the soil surface and space about 50 cm apart. Don't water too heavily until the plant is well developed. This plant does best in the tropics or warm temperate regions where plenty of water is available. In cooler climates, plant in a large pot containing a good, humus-rich potting mix. Water, and enclose the whole pot in a large plastic bag until the first strong shoots appear. Remove the plastic bag. Keep the soil moist and the pot in a warm,

sunny position away from cold winds. Ginger is a heavy feeder, so no matter where it is grown, it will need regular additions of manure. In late summer, after about five months growth, fresh green rhizomes are harvested. These are used fresh in cooking. In autumn, when leaves start to yellow and growth slows, roots

are harvested for slicing and drying. Dig the entire root but save some pieces for replanting. Ginger can be stored for several weeks in a sealed plastic bag in the refrigerator. It can also be frozen. The pungency often depends on the climate and soil in which the rhizome is grown.

Use The pungent, spicy rhizome is the part eaten. Ginger rhizomes can be sliced, shredded, pickled and candied or dried and ground. They are used in curries, sauces and chutneys. Fresh rhizomes are also used to manufacture ginger ale. If buying ginger rhizomes, look for two different sorts, young and old. Both should be plump with no bruises. Young ginger has pale yellow, thin skin with pink shoots. Older ginger is browner with a thicker skin that needs to be removed before use. These rhizomes are usually used in cooked dishes and added at the beginning of cooking to allow the flavours to infuse though the dish. Asian chefs often use ginger to disguise strong fishy flavours and to counterbalance strong fatty meat flavours. Young ginger is better for grating and pounding, and is used to extract the juice used as a marinade in some Chinese dishes. It can also be eaten raw. In some parts of South-East Asia, the leafstalks too are an important flavouring. Larger leaves are often used to wrap food that is then steamed or boiled. Ginger is also an important medicinal plant and is taken to treat colds and chills, as a circulatory stimulant, to improve digestion and for motion sickness. Many cultures also believe that it is aphrodisiac.

References and further reading

References marked with an * contain numerous recipes.

*Brissenden, R., *South East Asian Food*, Penguin Books Australia Ltd, Ringwood, Victoria, Australia, 1996.

*Chin, H. F., *Malaysian Vegetables in Colour, A Complete Guide*, Tropical Press, Kuala Lumpur, Malaysia, 1999.

*Dahlen, M. & Phillipps, K., *A Popular Guide to Chinese Vegetables*, MPH Bookstores, Singapore, 1982.

Exotic Greens, A selection of Vietnamese herbs, vegetables, recipes and remedies from the Collingwood Community Gardens, Coll-LINK, Abbotsford, Victoria, 1998.

Facciola, S., *Cornucopia II, A Sourcebook of Edible Plants*, Kampong Publications, Vista, California, USA, 1998.

*Freeman, M. & Le Van Nhan, *The Vietnamese Cookbook*, Viking Press, 1995.

*Harrington, G., *Grow Your Own Chinese Vegetables*, Gardenway Publishing, Pownal, Vermont, USA, 1978.

Herklots, G. A. C., *Vegetables in South-East Asia*, George Allen and Unwin Ltd, London, United Kingdom, 1972.

Hutton, W., *Tropical Herbs and Spices of Thailand*, Asia Books, Bangkok, 1997.

Jacquat, C., *Plants from the Markets of Thailand*, D.K. Bookhouse, Bangkok, Thailand.

*Jaffrey, M., *Madhur Jaffrey's World Vegetarian*, Edbury Press, London, 1998.

*Kong Foong Ling, *The Food of Asia: Authentic Recipes from China, India, Indonesia, Japan, Singapore, Malaysia, Thailand and Vietnam*, Periplus World Cookbooks, New York, 1998.

*Larkcom, J., *Oriental Vegetables, The Complete Guide for Garden and Kitchen*, John Murray (Publishers) Ltd, London, 1991.

Macmillan, H. F., *Tropical Planting and Gardening*, fifth edition, Macmillan & Co Ltd, New York, 1956.

Nguyen, V. Q., *Growing Asian vegetables*, Agfact H8.1.37, first edition 1992., N.S.W Agriculture.

*Passmore, J., *The Encyclopedia of Asian Food and Cooking*, Doubleday, Sydney, Australia, 1992.

Phillips, R. & Rix, M., *Vegetables*, Pan Macmillan Publishers, London, 1993.

Smith, K., *Growing Uncommon Fruits and Vegetables in Australia*, New Holland Publishers Pty Ltd, Frenchs Forest, NSW, Australia, 1998.

*Solomon, C., *Charmaine Solomon's Thai Cookbook*, Greenhouse Publications, Elwood, Victoria, Australia 1989.

*Solomon, C., *Encyclopaedia of Asian Food* Periplus, New York 1996.

Waters, C. T., Morgan, W. C. & McGeary, D. J., *Oriental Vegetables*, Agmedia, East Melbourne, Victoria, Australia, 1992.

Useful Internet sites

http://www.hort.purdue.edu/newcrop/default.html
The Web site of the Center for New Crops & Plant Products at Purdue University.

http://www.uq.edu.au/~gagkrego/index.htm
The Australian New Crops Home Page

http://www.dce.vic.gov.au/trade/asiaveg/aa-home.htm
Access to Asian Vegetables.
Agriculture & Food Initiative (AFI) and the Rural Industries Research & Development Corporation (RIRDC)

http://www.rirdc.gov.au/programs/af.html
Rural Industries Research & Development Corporation
Our Research Programs: Asian Foods

http://www.earthcare.com.au/default.htm
*Bamboo, aquatic plants, ginger, spices and more.
A nursery and farm based in the Sunshine Coast Hinterland, Queensland.

http://www.scs.leeds.ac.uk/pfaf/index.html
Plants for a Future. A Resource and Information Centre for Edible and other useful plants

http://www.sci-ctr.edu.sg/ssc/publication/veg/contents.html
A Guide To Common Vegetables The Singapore Science Centre
This guide features a wide range of vegetables available in the local wet markets and gives a description accompanied by illustrations and photographs of each vegetable.

http://www.sintercom.org/makan/recipes.htm
*Hundreds of recipes from many different Asian countries and much more information about food and sources.

Mail order suppliers of Asian herb and vegetable seeds and plants

Bay Seed Garden
PO Box 715, Busselton. WA 6280
(08) 9752 2513
Organic seeds

Digger's Seeds
105 Latrobe Parade, Dromana, 3936
(03) 5987 1877, fax (03) 5981 4298
email: orders@diggers.com.au
Seeds, plants, books, hardware

Earthcare Enterprises
PO Box 500, Maleny, Qld 4552
(07) 5494 4666
email: webmaster@earthcare.com.au
web site: http://www.earthcare.com.au/default.htm
Plants and seeds

Eden Seeds and Books
MS 316, Gympie, NSW 4570
(07) 5486 5230, freecall 1800 188 199, fax(07) 5486 5586
Seeds, plants and books

Green Harvest
52 Crystal Waters Permaculture Village, MS 16, via Maleny, Qld 4552
(07) 5494 4676, fax (07) 5494 4674
email: greenhar@ozemail.com.au
Seeds, plants, books, hardware.

Greenpatch Organic Seeds
PO Box 1285, Taree, NSW 2430
Tel/fax (02) 6551 4240
Non-hybrid, open pollinated seed, plants and books

Kings Herb Seeds
PO Box 975, Penrith, NSW 2751
(02) 4776 1493
Seeds

Minara Pty Ltd.
25 Centurion St, Bridgeman Downs, Qld 4035
Tel (07) 3263 4090, fax (07) 3263 3182
Seeds

New Gippsland Seeds and Bulbs
PO Box 1, Silvan, 3795
(03) 9737 9560, fax (03) 9737 9292
email: newgipps@bigpond.com
web site: www.possumpages.com.au/
newgipps/
Seeds, bulbs and books

Phoenix Seeds
PO Box 207, Snug, Tas 7054
(03) 6267 9663, fax (03) 6267 9592
Seeds, plants and books

Shipard's Herb Farm
Box 66, Nambour, Qld 4560
(07) 5441 1101
Plants and books

Other useful addresses

The Heritage Seed Curators of Australia
P O Box 1450
Bairnsdale, Vic 3875
email: han.HSCA@b150.aone.net.au
web site: www.ozemail.com.au/~hsca

The Seed Savers Network
PO Box 975, Byron Bay, NSW 2481

Index